Pichifkes

Stories heard On the Road and By the Way

by

HANOCH TELLER

New York City Publishing Company

ISBN 0-9614772-7-X

Registered in Library of Congress

12 11 10 9 8 7 6 5 4 3 2

Distributed by:
FELDHEIM PUBLISHERS
200 Airport Executive Park
Spring Valley, NY 10977

J. Lehmann
Hebrew Booksellers
20 Cambridge Terrace
Gateshead
Tyne & Wear

This edition of *Pichifkes*
was produced especially for NCSY

— *the moving force of the teshuvah movement*

• **NCSY** pioneered and gave rise to the near miraculous phenomenon of thousands of young Jews, intelligent and accomplished, searching and yearning for spirituality, Torah and roots.

• **NCSY** inspires more young people to become Sabbath observers than any other institution or program in North America and Jewish life.

• **NCSY** has given rise to a special group of yeshivos in the United States and Israel for the newly observant.

• **NCSY** serves as the only outreach program in scores of American and Canadian communities.

• **NCSY**, one of the largest and most effective Jewish movements in the world — a powerful and effective force for Jewish survival, revival and return — urgently requires your commitment and support in order to maintain and expand its activities and programs.

For further information contact:
NATIONAL CONFERENCE OF SYNAGOGUE YOUTH
70 West 36th Street
New York, NY 10018
(212) 244-2011 • Fax (212) 268-4819

NCSY — The Youth Movement of the Orthodox Union

In loving memory of

M. Manuel Merzon

Advocate for his People

A husband, a father, a teacher, and a leader, Manuel Merzon was all. An incisive legal expert, he was not above straightening up the shul after service. He was not the caretaker of the synagogue, but he took care that all of the lessons and concepts he absorbed in the *mikdash me'at* were widely disseminated.

He saw to it that every will drafted for a Jewish client included a clause for charitable contributions, and similar guarantees regarding Torah education for the deceased's heirs. His legal fee from a local rabbi was the latter's consent to learn with him *b'chevrusa*, a partnership that spanned over two decades.

Whether away or at home, his dedication to Torah study was staggering. His Florida vacation was dedicated solely to learning in the hotel's air-conditioned shul.

His innate sensitivity to justice far exceeded his professional training. He allowed himself no respite when it came to activism for Soviet Jewry, battling assimilation, seeking retribution against the enemies of our People, and helping fellow Jews in distress.

Just as he provided legal aid gratis for the needy, he likewise donated his talents for any worthy cause, be it writing a weekly newspaper column on Torah insights or managing the local Jewish cemetery.

His very appearance in court proved to be a glorification of God's holy Name for Jew and gentile alike. He never failed to wear his *kipah* there and demonstrate the fear of Heaven it symbolizes.

May his memory be a blessing and an inspiration.

משה בן מנחם מענדל זצ"ל

נלב"ע ח"י טבת תשמ"ח

ת.נ.צ.ב.ה.

Also by Hanoch Teller

Once Upon a Soul
Soul Survivors
'Souled!'
The Steipler Gaon
Sunset
Courtrooms of the Mind
Above the Bottom Line
The Bostoner
Bridges of Steel, Ladders of Gold

APPROBATION FROM HAGAON HARAV
CHAIM KREISWIRTH SHLITA

משרד הרבנות
על יד
הקהלה החרדית
מחזיקי הדת

ב"ה
אנטוּוערפּען,   תש
JACOB JACOBSSTRAAT, 22

הרב ר' הנוך העניך נ"י...

Contents

Preface

AFTER SEVERAL YEARS of writing and telling stories, it has become clear to me that people want a story with a minimum of loose ends, a tale that inspires, elucidates, and crystallizes its subject.

The storytellers I encounter are the kind of folk who take the fabric of life and fashion it into fascinating, significant episodes of Providence. They relate their stories in order to make sense out of the jumble of their experiences, and to acknowledge the peculiar and powerful moments that creep into the most humdrum existence. It is their way of revealing God's mighty hand, of imparting their love and ethics to their offspring and of having the last laugh on a sometimes cruel and always fickle fate.

The stories I write, or more accurately, "relate,"

are true in essence, although not always absolutely faithful to detail. I do not investigate the veracity of the storyteller; I do, however, research the historical background and setting of his tale. Every story has multiple layers of meaning and implication, which subtly twist and turn with the telling. Furthermore, every person hears a story differently. Thus, by the time I have heard, digested, interpreted, and retold a story, it may differ from the version others have heard. I have, in fact, received a few complaints on this score, but, *baruch Hashem*, at least as many compliments. Notwithstanding my tendency to take certain literary liberties in order to enhance a Torah lesson, many people have related stories of this genre to me and many of them have found their way into my works.

Many have not.

I have had occasion to reflect on this, usually at stop lights. Recently, when *Pichifkes* was in its gestation period, I screeched to a halt at one of Jerusalem's intersections. Clutch in, brake depressed, I suddenly realized a mistake I'd been making. In my search for thematically correlated stories with a message, I had neglected a treasure trove that Providence had placed in my path. People are constantly telling me their inspiring and emboldening stories, but those that do not fit into whatever I happen to be working on get consigned to the "*pichifkes* file" and are never shared with others.

To think that I'd been suppressing these gems! I cannot begin to describe my anxiety; I was haunted by a feeling that I had been tampering with destiny.

I suppose the traffic light changed then, the green arrow glowed, and I made my right turn. But the only thing I remember about the rest of that drive was my sudden compulsion to dash home and begin working assiduously on *Pichifkes.*

Many people helped me in my endeavors. I beg forgiveness of anyone I have inadvertently omitted from these acknowledgments: Yechiel Kapiloff, Chaim Meyerson, Isaac Elchonen Mozeson, Sarah Scheller, Daniel Taub, and Barbara Szenes. In the preface to *Above the Bottom Line,* I thanked Reb Leibel Estrin for his work and his indomitable faith. In this book, his work was even more indomitable and faithful. My gratitude to Marsi Tabak, who taught me how to write and still graciously repeats the lessons, exceeds the skill implanted. Thanks and gratitude are extended yet again to the dedicated team at NYC Publishing Co., and to Heidi Tenzer and the folks at *Jewish Action.*

The *roshei yeshiva* of the Bais Binyomin Yeshiva in Stamford, Connecticut, have inspired an elite corps of young men over the years. It has been my good fortune to also gain from their wisdom and influence. I single out Harav Dovid Hersh Mayer not only for teaching me how to appreciate and *daheir* a story, but for providing such deep insight into *zeh sefer toldos adam.*

Needless to say, I am grateful to all my *rebbeim*, especially those of the Mirrer Yeshiva where I learn.

I also thank my students, who have taught me far more (in academic and related fields) than I could possibly convey to them.

And, as ever, my dear friends who have helped me in various ways all have a share in that which I produce. I therefore thank Benjie and Sussie Brecher, Meyer and Leah Eichler, Yaakov and Pessy Florans, Dov and Bashie Goldbaum, Mendy and Nechama Itzinger, Chezky and Esther Paskesz, Yitzchok and Aliza Rosenberg, and Joseph and Devora Telushkin.

Before I declare my indebtedness to the Almighty, I wish to express my love and appreciation to two of His most pivotal partners, Mr. and Mrs. Shlomo Meir Teller, who happen to be the kind and patient parents of this author. I am equally blessed by their daughter-in-law, who enables me to do all that I can both on and off the road and by the way. Thank you, Hashem.

אילו פי מלא שירה וידי ידי סופר אמן, לא אספיק להודות
להשי"ת על כל החסד אשר חנני וההזדמנות לשתף את
הקוראים בחויותי.

Hanoch Teller
Jerusalem תו"י
Issru Chag HaSukkos 5750 / October 1989

Introduction

EXITING the jetway of Milwaukee's General Mitchell Field Airport slightly worse for the wear after a dispute with a fellow passenger over something terribly important that I can't recall, I noticed that my prearranged lift into town hadn't yet arrived. I repaired to the terminal lounge, where I went about my business — which at the time was a *gemara Bava Basra*.

I soon realized that I was being watched. The eyes of the watcher drew closer. I feigned concentration.

Unimpressed, my observer opened the discussion with an accusation: "How come all the good stories happen to you?" The questioner, a caustic, ancient (perhaps fifty-year-old) man with a face mobile enough to express twenty-three different grades of disgust, allowed me a millisecond to respond.

Since I couldn't press the buzzer fast enough, he continued to pepper me with questions, particularly concerning people's undisguised disinterest in *his* stories.

When he finally paused for station identification, I suggested that people aren't interested in commonplace events. Reality is confusing, tiresome, and lacking in impact. It often seems to turn out bad and we rarely understand why. It teaches us little — or it teaches us much, at great cost. Besides, why would a reader be interested in reality? He's got more than enough of his own.

The reader prefers an *extract* of reality, a tale that is focused and crystallized in such a way that it clarifies thoughts and expands the mind, or to put it more succinctly: a story that reveals an insight. Or better yet: *realism* as opposed to *reality*. A literary presentation that *seems* accurate has greater appeal than does absolute truth.

In the world of fiction writing this is known as the "Mack truck principle," which stipulates that the lazy writer is forbidden to resolve literary complications by having all his characters run over by Mack trucks, even though such things have been known to happen in *reality*. Lightning strokes are also taboo, and a pauper may not be rescued from his plight by fortuitously finding a winning lottery ticket. Although these phenomena do actually occur with relative frequency, including them in a plot destroys the *realistic feel* of the story.

In almost all of my writing, I have avoided both boring reality and fictitious realism, focusing instead on extraordinary people and events. Freed of the constraints of fiction-writing, I am able to record non-fiction riddled with Mack trucks, lightning strokes, and fortuitous finds, which the reader sees *not* as the literary devices of a lazy writer, but as the irrefutable evidence of Divine Providence they are.

Over the years, I have been privileged to witness and hear of countless gems, which I have meticulously stored away and labeled "Pichifkes" — a Yiddish colloquialism for "precious little curios." Having finally committed to paper some of these extraordinary incidents, I can only hope that *Pichifkes* will indeed present new insights into the outstanding character of God's Chosen People, a people whose desire to give and share should be an inspiration to us all.

It is difficult to apply a unifying theme to an anthology assembled from stories I have heard during my travels. Nevertheless the reader will discern — as I did — that the twin themes of *chessed* (human kindness) and *Hashgacha* (Divine Providence) dominate this volume, just as they do our outlook and behavior.

Every story in this book, like every one I have ever written or told, contains a lesson. If the reader can emerge from the anesthesia of our rather decadent society, which insidiously dulls the senses to the beauty and wonders the Almighty has graciously scattered throughout His world, the timeless lessons of these stories will be self-evident.

The stories in this volume have been divided into three sections, in accord with a Talmudic maxim: "In three ways is a man distinguished: by his voice, his appearance, and his knowledge" (*Sanhedrin* 38a). Although the Talmud goes on to explain why these distinctions are essential, I feel that they are particularly applicable to this book.

Voice creates a superficial impression: even if you have never met a person, you can get to know him casually through a mere telephone conversation.

Appearance, of course, creates a deeper, more lasting impression: facial expressions and gestures accompany the voice; attire and bearing speak volumes.

The most profound impression, however, is honed by cogitation and analysis. The opportunity to delve and ponder forges an image that is not quickly forgotten.

It is hoped that this division will maximize the impact of the stories in *Pichifkes*. The shortest ones, told virtually as they were heard on the road and by the way, can be found in the first chapter, **Voices**. Stories with greater development and description constitute the second chapter, **Visions**. The third chapter, **Vistas**, written in what has come to be known as "soul style," contains stories which it is hoped will stimulate all the senses and imprint their message permanently on the mind and heart of the reader. I pray that these diverse approaches will make all the stories "distinguished."

Voices

Voices

WHEN A NEW YORK housewife discovered that her butcher had forgotten to remove the skewer clips from the chicken he had barbequed for her, she placed the clips in a bag and sent them back to the store with her son. The butcher thanked the boy, and a minute later ran down the street after him to call him back. He placed the clips on the scale and then handed the boy fourteen cents to bring back to his mother.

All the touching acts of unrivalled courage and selfless devotion Dr. Elaine Nussbaum had witnessed in her career as a special education teacher paled alongside one remarkable instance of *hakkaras hatov*.

Under New York City regulations, which provide

for education for the housebound, Dr. Nussbaum was assigned to a family in a religious neighborhood of Brooklyn. Her student was a five-year-old girl suffering from a rare congenital defect that had claimed her mind. Lacking a nervous system and the ability to control her bodily functions, the child was only clinically alive.

Then as now, the girl lay in a crib festooned with brand-new toys that she would never appreciate. Indeed, expecting her to react to light, dark, heat, or cold, or even to raise a tiny pinky, would be tantamount to expecting a miracle.

During one session with her, Dr. Nussbaum was startled to meet the girl's father, who walked into the room and lovingly took his daughter in his arms. Unlike normal children, who are pliable and cuddly, this girl was rigid and unresponsive. But her proud parent seemed oblivious to that. Hugging and kissing his daughter, he turned to the specialist and beamed. "What do you say about our treasure?" he asked without irony. "Thank God! After fourteen miscarriages the Almighty was kind enough to bestow upon us this blessing!"

A rabbi in New York was asked one afternoon why all the "Peylim" posters indicate that the outreach organization has set up numerous learning centers in Israel. "After all, these learning groups don't function in Brooklyn," the questioner remarked.

"I guess," the rabbi replied, "they wish others to learn from their example."

Later that evening the rabbi's answer resounded in his ears, and the very next week he began teaching *mishnayos* to neighborhood children.

The rabbi of South Bend, Indiana, once travelled to the local hospital to comfort a family which had just suffered the loss of a close relative, and at the same time to ensure a halachic burial for the deceased.

One of the bereaved, however, objected to the rabbi's intervention. "No rabbi," he asserted, "is going to tell me about Jewish law. I saw the holiest of all rabbis suffer the greatest humiliation at the hands of the Nazis.

"In our village," he continued emotionally, "we were all rounded up and forced to spit at and slap the face of the rabbi. After that everyone was shot. I am the sole survivor of that town. Even the holy Rabbi Moshe Yitzchok does not have a living relative to tell his tale. What good did observing Jewish law do for him, I ask you?"

Retaining his composure, the rabbi informed the embittered man that he was wrong on two counts. The mourner sat up with visible indignation.

"First," the rabbi said, "the rav you're referring to was named Moshe *Yaakov*. And second, I should know, because I am his grandson and I was named after him."

The man literally slid under his chair. Needless to say, a proper funeral was arranged.

Ensign Jeff Winograd was serving his military stint on the aircraft carrier *USS John F. Kennedy.* One fateful afternoon he wandered into a restricted area of the carrier's deck... just as combat fighters were returning from an exercise. The awesome air currents generated by the jets were overwhelming, and Winograd was propelled overboard by one of the gusts.

A crewman who'd witnessed the freak accident immediately sounded the tocsin for a helicopter pilot to rescue the sailor who had plunged into the sea. The pilot in charge of retrieval missions could not be found, however — not in the cabin, in the engine room, on deck, or in the control tower. Unbeknownst to the seaman, the flyer he was looking for was none other than Ensign Winograd.

The commanding officer realized that every second counted. The chances of a man surviving a several-story fall into icy waters were not very good. A second pilot was dispatched and he managed to fish out the bobbing sailor, who had resolved in the interim that if he were to live through this ordeal, he would become the *Kennedy's* sole kosher, *shomer Shabbos* crewman, and thus he remains to this day.

Ｑ

A welfare recipient in New York once entered a 47th Street photo store and tried to sell the proprietor a pair of obviously purloined tefillin.

Berel, the *chassid* behind the counter, asked to see the merchandise. He gingerly removed the tefillin from their case and promptly declared: "Hey! What are you trying to do, cheat me? You've only got half a set here. Where's the one for the other arm?"

The thief looked bewildered and embarrassed. Berel told him that in this condition the goods weren't even worth two dollars but he would give him five for his trouble. The robber walked out of the store with the distinct impression that crime doesn't pay, and Berel quickly looked up the phone number of the person whose name was stitched into the tefillin bag.

The tables were turned on Jewish wit when a yeshiva student heading up to the Catskill Mountains stopped to help out a stranded *Yid*. But there was something about the hapless motorist that seemed a bit, well, un-Jewish.

When questioned about his curious appearance, the driver explained that he wasn't really Jewish, but he always kept a yarmulke in his glove compartment. It seems that he had been driving on this highway for many years, and no one had ever stopped to help him whenever he'd had a breakdown. He noticed, however, that anyone with a *kipah* always had but a brief wait before a coreligionist pulled over to lend a hand.

A young *chassid* blessed with a large family was once stopped by a German tourist and asked what right he had to bring so many children into a world where there isn't sufficient food to feed the hungry, and where the current population explosion is sure to cause drastic demographic problems. "You have a very good point," the *chassid* replied to the tourist, "and I promise to consider it after I have six million children."

Josh, a young Orthodox doctor from Chicago, was determined not to desecrate Shabbos during his internship. To this end, he took two valuable days off work to follow a lead on a possible *shomer Shabbos* internship in San Diego. Although he had no relatives or friends there, and San Diego seemed so remote, Shabbos, he reasoned, was infinitely more important than any social considerations.

Josh applied and, thanks to his credentials, was immediately accepted — at which point he felt it safe to broach the subject of Sabbath observance. His acceptance was quickly rescinded, and the young doctor had only a hefty airfare to show for his efforts.

Thoroughly frustrated, he slowly made his way out of the medical center. Shuffling his feet, he startled a friendly medical secretary, who looked up from her computer and asked, "What'sa matta, Doc? Yo' hand slip in surgery?" Her warm concern was just what the doctor ordered and Josh unburdened himself to this stranger.

"Don't worry 'bout nuthin'," she comforted him. "Befo' I got this here job I was a medical secretary on the East Coast in Brookdale, where all you guys with the caps don' work on Satidays."

With that, she picked up the telephone and dialed the chief resident. "Hey, babycakes," she fawned, twirling her necklace as she spoke, "this here's Cindy. Y'know, from upstairs? I need a great big favor for one o' my boyfriends, but it's really fo' yo' own good.

"Ya see, he's one of them guys don' work Satidays or Friday nights." She eyed her "boyfriend" for confirmation and the doctor nodded enthusiastically.

"But he'll work any ol' Sunday you please, Christmas and Easter, too. I knew I could depend on ya," she cooed without waiting for a reply. "I'm sendin' him right on down to ya. Bye, now."

Dear Chatzkal,

I regret what I said and the way I behaved.

I know I caused you hurt, but I was only reacting to the statement you made...

Yossi crumpled up the letter, took a new sheet of paper, and began his fourth attempt to speak his mind.

> Dear Chatzkal,
> I really should have known better. I shouldn't have blamed you for...

This, too, was tossed into the circular file.

Yossi's wife could not help but notice her husband's intense concentration, and asked him what he was doing.

Yossi reflected for a moment and then stoically responded that he was writing a letter.

"So what's the big fuss?" she asked.

"Because I have to make sure it's perfect. There can't be any misunderstandings this time." Armed with an even greater sense of purpose, he resumed his writing.

> Dear Chatzkal,
> I was wrong. If I would have only realized...

This draft, too, joined its companions in the wastebasket. Reduced to stony silence, Yossi buried his head in his arms and fixed his every thought on what was rapidly becoming a dead letter.

At last he sat up, grabbed a new piece of paper, and began,

Dear Chatzkal,

I apologize with all my heart and with every fiber of my being. I love you.

Your friend,

Yossi

Resolved that he had completed his mission, he got up from his desk. His wife asked if he could take some things along with him if he was headed for the mailbox. "I'm taking a different route," he explained. "I have to make this a personal delivery."

Unwilling to banish such a precious piece of paper to his pocket, Yossi clutched the letter in his hand. He boarded a bus to the outskirts of town and got off at the last stop. Somberly, Yossi made his way down the hill and his eyes began to swim.

Deliberately maneuvering his way, he finally reached Chatzkal and placed the letter on top of the fresh grave.

Once, when I was flying from Chicago to Pittsburgh, I was joined in the aisle by an air corpsman with a gladiatorial physique. His imposing dimensions were adequate to insure I would be on my best behavior.

Shortly after we were airborne I noticed that he had wings, that is, the insignia of a pilot, so I seized the opportunity to solve a riddle that had puzzled me on dozens of flights. "Why is it," I asked, "that whenever a flight is significantly delayed, the captain announces over the P.A. system that he is requesting 'direct routing'? Wouldn't the plane *normally* fly 'direct'? Isn't the shortest distance in the air the same as on the ground — a straight line?"

Before offering an answer, my neighbor sized me up. He looked at my *kipah* and at the *sefer* I was studying before focusing directly on me. "There are roadways in the sky," he began, "not all that different from the highways on the ground. To avoid congestion and possible hazards, a plane may not fly a straight line, but must stick to a flight plan directed by ground control, which is inevitably indirect.

"When a flight is very late in departing," he went on, "the pilot may request 'direct routing' to make up for lost time. It is up to the tower to see if such an option is feasible by checking with all the other flight plans simultaneously scheduled to cover the same area."

The airman noticed that I was drifting off in thought. "What's the matter?" he asked. I couldn't disguise my astonishment.

"I have travelled across America teaching — and hopefully inspiring — my brethren. Jews throughout the country wish to embrace their religion but suffer from a late start and all kinds of hardships that impede observance."

I stopped myself in mid-thought. Why was I sharing my personal, parochial reflections with this gentile stranger?

"Keep going," he ordered in a voice as commanding as a drill sergeant's.

I cowered and hastily obliged. "Well, I was wondering if God, seeing how great is the thirst but how languid the fulfillment, could order 'direct routing' for American Jewry's return flight."

"Where are you speaking tonight?" the pilot asked.

"Why?" I spluttered back.

"Because that's the second-best question I've ever heard."

More confounded than before, I asked, "What is the first?"

He smiled sheepishly, relaxed his rigid exclamation-point posture, and suddenly appeared far more like a young teenager than a brawny combat pilot. "My favorite question," he said at last, "is *Mah nishtanah halailah hazeh mikol halailos?*"

Visions

Ticket to Ride

ONE EVENING, a young man learning in a Midwest *kollel* sought to pay a condolence call on his landlord, who lived in what was once the city's Jewish neighborhood. The neighbohood had since deteriorated and become a high-crime area. The mourner, not a religious man, was not at home when the young man arrived but was due to return any minute. "Any minute" stretched into half an hour, and the student began to fidget with anxiety.

That particular evening was the one night on which he routinely delivered a weekly *shiur* to the local *baalei battim,* and the hour of the class was rapidly approaching. He sincerely wished to wait for his landlord and personally express his sympathy, but at the same time he had a responsibility to the community.

With no alternative, he rose to leave just as his

landlord returned home. The uneasy student stayed to comfort the bereaved for five minutes and then excused himself. At this point his chances of making it to the *shiur* on time were slim. He had already given up on calling a cab company since it would have taken at least fifteen minutes for the taxi to arrive. His only hope was to try and hail a hack on the street.

I N THAT NEIGHBORHOOD, finding a cruising cab was highly unlikely. Hoping for the best, the scholar dashed outside, and witnessed a scene more typical of rural America than an urban metropolis: not a single pedestrian was in sight, let alone a motor vehicle; a lone Chihuahua was the only living thing to grace the deserted street. Dismayed, he prayed out loud, "O Lord, this is a matter of *talmud Torah d'rabbim*! Please help me!"

No sooner had he uttered his plea than a taxi pulled up across the street and let off a hirsute hippy. The student waved excitedly at this Godsend and the cabbie catapulted over to the frantic gesticulator.

Any "Yellow" patron can confirm that part of any taxi driver's uniform is a stoic expression that doesn't leave his face from the moment he gets behind the wheel until he ends his shift. But this cabbie's countenance shone with amazement; genuine emotion danced all over his features.

"Ya ain't gonna believe dis," he declared to his pious passenger. "Dis is da weirdest ting dat ever did happen t'me. Ya seez dat guy just got out? He tells me take him t'da lake for ten bucks.

"I tells him ten bucks ain't 'nuf no how t'get to da lake. So he sez, 'Den take me as far as ya can fer ten bucks.' An' here we iz, an' here you iz, wavin' an' flaggin' me down. An' me, I'm figurin' on ridin' back empty an' blowin' da whole dang night wid no payin' fare. Whacha doin' waitin' anyways? You neva git a cab t'come way out here, no way, Jose."

The young man replied simply, "God sent you."

"Uh-oh, you one a' dem religious fan-attix or sumpin?"

"I'm telling you," the Jew insisted, "God sent you."

The driver stared pensively into the rearview mirror for a moment. "Ya know," he said in a hesitant tone, "maybe youze right. Cuz when it come to payin', dis guy give me a fifty an' akses fer change. Fifty bucks woulda got him t'da lake and back, you betcha black hat it woulda."

Heard from: Shraga Wahlstein

Public Servant

ENACHEM Dovid Felstein, *z"l*, modest diamond merchant and logician of sorts, believed that the quintessence of model behavior was sparing a fellow human being from viewing his own flaws. His credo was an extension of the well-known Slabodka motto: "The world was created for me." He would have phrased it, "I was created to enable others to enjoy *their* world."

Menachem Dovid obviously came to this conclusion at an early age. When he was just sixteen and his friends were advancing to *yeshiva gedolah*, Felstein, of his own volition, left yeshiva (but not learning) to aid his ailing father at work.

By the time he was married, Menachem had finely tuned his *weltanschauung* and found it innumerable applications. Installed within his sensitivity antennae was a special sensor that was activated every time someone told an unfunny joke. Strange that a man imbued with an extraordinarily sharp wit should find these pathetic attempts at humor so amusing. In fact, what really wasn't funny from Menachem Dovid's perspective was the shame and embarrassment that results from failed efforts to entertain. Therefore, as long as the diamantaire was present, uncontrollable peals of laughter poured forth, and no one suffered this hurt.

Felstein similarly understood the sensitive soul of the itinerant merchant. No matter what a peddler was peddling, Menachem Dovid always seemed to need an inordinate quantity of it. Accordingly, not only did he provide some long-sought-after business, but he heaped gratitude upon the merchant for being so kind as to visit his town. Any given week, Felstein purchased dozens of useless items from peddlers who had traversed hill and dale without landing a single sale. Terrarium construction kits, filter modulators for outdoor pools, contoured maps of footpaths in the Adirondacks — he considered all these knickknacks very valuable, for they enabled a fellow Jew to earn his livelihood with dignity.

FOR TWENTY YEARS Mr. Felstein ate lunch at the same restaurant. Moreover, despite the many sumptuous dishes available, his order never varied: a small serving of fish and a vegetable.

Lest one draw the wrong conclusion, Felstein's dietary cravings did not favor fish to the exclusion of all the other entries on the menu. Indeed, his wife asserted that in seventy years he had never uttered a single comment germane to his appetite. This soft-spoken abstemiousness, however, was restricted to his own table.

Whenever Menachem Dovid found himself at a *simcha* or at someone else's house, he just couldn't seem to get enough of whatever was being served. Massive quantities were consumed by this gastronomically diffident man — to the utter delight of his hosts.

At one particular bar mitzva the food contributed little to the festive atmosphere. As if rehearsed, each guest took but one bite of his serving before pushing the plate to a safe distance. Menachem Felstein, however, was seen hailing the waiter for a hearty second helping — just as the *baal hasimcha* passed by.

I N GOOD TIMES and bad, Menachem Dovid's commitment to guarding the feelings of others was steadfast. Rabbi Michoel Ber Weissmandel, a regular breakfast guest of the generous merchant, learned this the morning he was awakened with the tragic news that the Felsteins' daughter, a mother of several children, had died.

At first Reb Michoel Ber figured that this was no time to break bread with his hosts. But on second thought he reasoned that now more than ever, his presence was needed. Rabbi Weissmandel was not sure if the Felsteins were even aware of the tragedy and he feared that he might have the unpleasant task of bearing the tidings.

Obviously they had not been informed, for he was greeted with the same cheery "good morning" as always. Rabbi Weissmandel had little time to ponder how to break the news for he was immediately seated and served. "Better that I wait until after breakfast," the rabbi concluded, and mournfully consumed the meal. Only after Reb Michoel Ber had finished *bentching* did the Felsteins begin to weep uncontrollably; somehow they had managed to contain their grief so as not to disturb the rabbi's breakfast.

HOW CAN a person committed to sparing others hurt deliver *mussar*, which ineluctably entails highlighting a fault, a sure catalyst for humiliation and pain? Felstein submitted the problem to his cerebrum's research department and came up with a special formula, which went like this:

Before mentioning the area of improvement, he employed deep, relaxing ego massages, which primed the subject for the forthcoming rebuke while simultaneously highlighting how inappropriate it was for a person of such noble character to slip.

Thus it was standard procedure for him to first extoll the act he was about to criticize and to offer half a dozen vital justifications (which, of course, the perpetrator had never thought of) for such behavior. After Felstein had portrayed the action under discussion as the most magnanimous, philanthropic, and virtuous deed ever performed, he proceeded to compliment the guilty party. He never failed to mention that the subject of his *mussar* was not only a pious individual but, above all, a person who aspired to greatness. Then, and only then, came the rebuke.

Needless to say, Menachem Dovid could have asked for anything by that time — from a large sum of money to a personality overhaul — and the subject would have gladly provided it. But instead, this master of the human psyche merely requested more sensitivity in the future and a moratorium on hurtful deeds.

The *mussar* worked. Indeed, it got to the point where people contemplated erring just to entitle themselves to some of Felstein's delightful approach.

S INCE MENACHEM'S policy of justifying the behavior of others was well-known, he was once asked — half in jest — to vindicate the conduct of a rather insufferable rabbi.

Well-known and widely despised, Rabbi Plony found cause to deliver a protracted sermon at any and every occasion. He also insisted that these marathon monologues be heard by all and sundry. But this is not why a committee approached Mr. Find-Good-in-Others. They felt that attending the sermons, if you pushed patience and good manners to the hilt, was conceivably tolerable.

What they found absolutely, excruciatingly unbearable was Plony's tendency to lace each and every one of his sermons with repugnant, cacophonous *krechtzes*. "To sit through 14K bytes of Plony's random access memory on exegesis, hermeneutics, and eschatological excess is bad enough," they kvetched. "Must we suffer through such melodramatic accentuations as well?"

Menachem Dovid didn't hesitate for a moment with his response. "Obviously," he stated, as if he were privy to some easily obtainable information, "during the course of his talk he cannot help but recall the six perpetual *mitzvos* one is always obliged to bear in mind. Think about it: *Oy* — *aleph, vav, yud* — is a mnemonic device for each mitzva." And off the top of his head he proved how each mitzva was indeed hinted at by *Oy*.

Felstein grew pensive and then added wistfully, "I wish I would always bear those thoughts in mind."

But of course Menachem Dovid Felstein was on a level all by himself. An unassuming lay person without so much as a beard, he was the confidant of some of the most outstanding Torah personalities of this generation. Rabbis, scholars, and simple folk eagerly sought his company; it was the best way to feel good about themselves.

Heard from: Rabbi Zvi Dovidowitz

Mrs. Perlstein's Appointment

THERE is a certain Dr. Sternfeld in the Midwest whom I keep hearing stories about. Some anecdotes bear out his chronic, almost preternatural forgetfulness when it comes to billing needy clients, others confirm his redoubtable medical expertise, but all of them testify to his unmatched devotion to his patients. Considerate deeds and gestures that one wouldn't expect even from family are daily performed by Dr. Sternfeld as a matter of standard procedure.

Now this fellow is definitely worth a story, I thought. But then again, what is so special about a doctor being a good doctor — even if he's skilled, honest, giving, and sincere? The man's legendary humility compounded the difficulty of including a Dr. Sternfeld story in this volume... until a friend related the following gem:

ACERTAIN Mrs. Perlstein would visit Dr. Sternfeld periodically, seeking relief from one of her imaginary ailments. The doctor always made time for her and patiently listened to her tale of woe, punctuated by several well-placed *krechtzes*. He then diagnosed her problem with some impressive-sounding medicalese, which usually kept her content for two or three days. Thereupon she would return, complaining of yet another elusive illness. All too often she came to seek the free medical advice and/or sympathetic ear that so many others, professional or not, would never offer her.

One day a fellow named Jack spotted her returning to Dr. Sternfeld's office in the evening. Jack had escorted his daughter to a checkup with Dr. Sternfeld just that morning, and seeing the Royal Queen of Nudnicks twice in one day was too much!

Jack was incensed that she could bother the good doctor in the morning and then rob him of his precious evening hours, too. And all to treat her hypochondriacal pain — gratis! This was going too far! With clenched teeth and as much emotional restraint as he could muster, Jack asked Mrs. Perlstein what she was doing in the physician's office.

"**W**HY, I'm waiting for the doctor," she said indignantly. "What else would I be doing in a doctor's office?"

"But you were just here this morning!" Jack blurted out.

For once, the loquacious Mrs. Perlstein was silent.

"*Nuuuuu?*" Jack demanded.

"What are you, Dr. Sternfeld's secretary?" the peeved patient finally shot back. "I never saw you work here before, and if he did hire someone so rude, I am going to recommend that he dismiss you!"

"Fair enough. Now just answer the question!"

"Well, if you must know," Mrs. Perlstein countered, self-righteousness dripping from every syllable, "I have an appointment."

As it happened, Jack was privy to the fact that his had been the last appointment of the day. He had even seen Dr. Sternfeld packing up when he'd left the office.

"An appointment, huh?" he muttered in disgust.

"That's right," she said, thoroughly affronted. "Every Wednesday night I take the doctor out shopping. He drives me in exchange for my pointing out to him what items are worth purchasing..."

A T THAT VERY MOMENT Dr. Sternfeld emerged from his office, offering his geriatric date a gentleman's bow. With her head held high and her nose in the air, Mrs. Perlstein clutched her massive pocketbook, turned to Dr. Sternfeld with a "shall we?" look, and glared a condescending "I told you so!" at her detractor. Jack stood agog in the foyer, his jaw gaping in surprise, humility, and no small measure of awe.

Heard from: Dr. Yossi and Sarah Scheller

Her Worth is More Precious Than Pearls

ONE ASPECT of the human psyche exploited by poets and politicians, dissidents and demagogues is that every man wants a place he can call home. Of course, everyone has his own concept of home. To some it is a magnificent manse spread over an ample plot of land, to others a four-room urban apartment; for the more eccentric it may be a houseboat, or a bench in Grand Central Station. Regardless, a problem arises when one's concept of home does not match what is provided.

Mrs. Miriam Laster already had a place she could call home in the Boro Park section of Brooklyn, yet she discovered and developed an additional one in downtown Manhattan. For all intents and purposes, the sprawling New York University Medical Center is the Lasters' second home. Miriam walks in as if she owns it, and the hospital's thousands of employees address her as if her attitude were legitimately founded.

This tiny wisp of a woman, now in her seventies, did not acquire this prime Big Apple real estate because of her vast wealth or multiple holdings; Mrs. Laster is a woman rich in everything but money. It is her other assets that opened the doors to this hospital and other medical facilities as well.

As director of the Ramtas *bikur cholim* group, she worries about a lot more than just visiting the sick. Mrs. Laster's primary concern is patient care. Years ago she discovered that what is available is not always provided and what is provided is not always on par with what is available. Enter Miriam Laster.

A TIRELESS patient activist, she personally sees to it that her coreligionists are afforded the very best medical care. Mrs. Laster safeguards this standard by several means, but the most powerful weapon in her arsenal is the respect she commands.

At any hour of day or night, she is impeccably dressed and ready to visit any specialist or administrator in order to intercede on behalf of a patient. An array of fresh, homemade cakes are also on hand at all times for deposit with doctors' receptionists in exchange for entry into their inner sanctum.

Officially, Mrs. Laster runs a kindergarten, but this is merely a springboard from which to launch her operations. Since she's on call around the clock, the kindergarten is a convenient place to find her during the morning. Needless to say, none of her volunteer work is limited to daytime hours.

One associate tells of the time Mrs. Laster called him up at two o'clock in the morning and insisted that he drive her to NYU right away. Knowing enough not to ask, protest, or even suggest that the matter be dealt with in the morning, he dutifully complied with her typically peculiar request.

The cause of the emergency, he later learned, was Mrs. Laster's concern that a certain night staff had not been instructed to provide special accommodations for one of "her" patients. The *bikur cholim* director could neither relax nor wait just five more hours until she was assured the best care. Which brings us to the point of this story.

MAN WILL GO to great lengths and tremendous expense to maintain his health. In certain seemingly tragic instances the efforts, from our limited vantage point, appear to have been in vain and the family's grief is compounded by their costly expenditures. For those who have helped and offered their services, it is another sobering lesson in man's meager ability to deal with mortality.

Nonetheless, Mrs. Laster is never content that she has done enough. Maybe just a little more effort, she reasons, will generate the Divine compassion necessary to alter God's decree. And even when nothing more can be done, her mind still gropes and contrives. An illustration follows.

Yisrael Levine was the embodiment of the Russian *teshuva* movement, religious zeal, and the limits of human suffering. He was also plagued, among other ailments, with cancer of the liver. It was Yisrael's tenacity that had enabled him to survive his torturous stint in Siberia before winning passage to Israel. It was thus no surprise that even though his body was wracked with the pain of an "incurable" disease, he refused to give up. Without family, he faced a lonely fight for his life. Until he found an ally in Miriam Laster.

Armed with only a *Tehillim* and the address of a kindergarten in Brooklyn, Yisrael departed for America in search of advanced treatment. Mrs. Laster arranged appointments for him with top specialists who, aside from their expertise, were known to take on even the most dismal cases.

But for all her influence, Mrs. Laster could not find a single doctor willing to treat Levine. Yisrael's condition had deteriorated so much, the physicians argued, that any kind of treatment was not only useless but indefensibly cruel. His life expectancy was estimated at a matter of days. Even more than Yisrael Levine himself, who had lived a life of deaths, Mrs. Laster was crushed by the prognosis.

Reb Yisrael decided that it was only appropriate for him to spend his remaining moments in Eretz Yisrael, and to let his soul expire on holy ground. But this was hardly a consolation for Mrs. Laster.

The poor man had travelled all the way to America only to learn that his efforts had been in vain. She just couldn't let him leave unceremoniously, and she didn't.

NO TORAH GIANT or, *lehavdil*, celebrity ever received such an escort. The indefatigable Mrs. Laster arranged that every friend, companion, and acquaintance of Levine's in the States — plus each one's family — was there at the airport to bid him farewell. To lend prestige to the crowd and to award this noble Jew the respect he richly deserved, she also invited the major *roshei yeshiva* and scholars of the New York metropolitan area to be on hand. Addresses extolling Levine's virtues and prayers on his behalf followed one after another, and the stoic Reb Yisrael was touched as never before.

Tears streamed uncontrollably down Yisrael's pale, emaciated cheeks. He no longer had the strength to speak to those who had gathered, but he motioned his gratitude with a limp hand and moist eyes. This was to be his final *shalom* and he would cherish its every moment until being summoned to the Heavenly Assembly. The *roshei yeshiva*, the well-wishers, and even several gentile onlookers were crying as the wheelchair was pushed toward the departure terminal. All of a sudden the highly emotional scene appeared headed for a tragic conclusion as Reb Yisrael approached check-in.

Mrs. Laster insisted that he fly home first class, not only because it would be immeasurably easier for him, but because he deserved nothing less. As it turned out, however, arranging luxurious accommodations was the least of her problems.

The check-in hostess took one look at Yisrael Levine's slight, frail frame and thin skin, yellowed by liver cancer, and informed Mrs. Laster that she could not allow this man to board, first class or economy. Airlines have a regulation that anyone who appears too ill to fly may not travel.

Those observing the check-in counter from afar could not tell what was transpiring. They saw only an animated discussion under way, frequently punctuated by the hostess shaking her head. Suddenly, the debate came to an end and a boarding pass was handed to Mrs. Laster.

Only the most perspicacious observer would have noticed the transaction that preceded this dramatic turnaround. Discreetly, without attracting any attention, Mrs. Laster removed her long pearl necklace and all the other fine jewelry she had been wearing and slipped them to the hostess. The woman behind the counter swallowed wordlessly, inserted the precious items into her pocket, and started punching keys.

As always, Mrs. Laster gave it her all.

Heard from: Rabbi Michel Gutfarb and Mrs. Feigie Aryeh

Package Deal

ITH THE PASSING of their father, Yisrael, Zev, and Aliza Stein inherited a 40,000-shekel debt and a week of mournful togetherness in their dear departed's rented apartment. Whereas family tragedies usually have a way of uniting family members, senior Stein's death veered from this commonplace.

Yisrael and Zev had never been close, but at least they put up a cordial front. In that house of mourning, however, something turned the relationship irremediably sour, and neither their wives nor Aliza could dislodge the wedge that was driven between the two brothers.

They say time heals all wounds, but not this one. For three decades, relations stood at a standstill of dissociation and non-communication. Over the years, influential outsiders sought to catalyze a reconciliation, or at least an understanding — but to no avail.

IRONICALLY, when one of the warring parties finally made a noble attempt at brotherhood, the impetus came from within. Yisrael had the distinct "privilege" of chairing a tenants' committee meeting in his Jerusalem apartment building. The committee was charged with overseeing building maintenance and collecting the dues used to finance these repairs. Although this may sound like a prosaic enough activity, such meetings are generally convened atop a powderkeg of emotions. The confab in Yisrael's modest home was no different. In minutes it turned riotous, with tempers flaring, accusations flying, and insults rising to a crescendo of disharmony and bedlam.

Perching himself on top of a chair, Yisrael issued an earnest plea for peace. For three straight minutes he lectured a suddenly attentive audience on both the virtue and the utilitarian advantage of *shalom*. "God's name is peace," he concluded dramatically. "Let us not desecrate His holy name." With that, order was restored.

Suddenly a light bulb illuminated in his head. Not only does charity begin at home, a sobered Yisrael Stein pondered, but peace must as well. If he made no diplomatic overture towards his brother now, his inner voice instructed, then he would be guilty of felonious hypocrisy. But how? Thirty years of animosity had fortified, not softened, the enmity between Zev and himself.

Before Yisrael could think of an appropriate gesture, the calendar suggested one for him. In eleven days was Purim, the holiday of charity and friendship. With wholehearted fraternity, Yisrael Stein overcame his well-harbored scorn and lovingly assembled a package of *mishloach manos* for his estranged brother.

Yisrael's nine-year-old son, Avner, was to be the courier and his father impressed upon him the importance of this task. Purim only came once a year so the opportunity had to be seized now. By the time Avner left the house, it had become dazzlingly clear to him that no *mishloach manos* delivery he would ever make would be as significant as this one.

OBVIOUSLY, the assignment was not destined to be uneventful, for as the young boy alighted from the bus he tripped over some bricks discarded from a nearby construction site, and his precious cargo went sailing into the mud. Avner didn't know what to do. After his father's stern warning he was petrified to return home with the package in shambles. Thus, Avner Stein did what any conscientious nine-year-old in his situation might have done.

He gathered all the contents of the *mishloach manos* — dirt-coated chocolate, chocolate-coated dirt, broken bottles, and wine-soaked cookies — clumps of mud of various consistencies et all, and reinserted them in what was left of their ripped box. Fortunately, he figured, the name of the sender had not sustained any damage. Like a good little soldier, Avner Stein completed his mission.

When Zev Stein discovered the garbage his brother had sent him, he didn't view it as a Purim jest. In fact, the pitiful peace offering became a provocation and he felt obliged to respond in kind and at the same time one up him. Mud was the least of the trash Zev Stein dispatched to his brother.

Suffice it to say that it wasn't a merry Purim for the greater Stein family.

A YEAR came and went and Yisrael was no longer overcome with pangs of conscience and coexistence. Indeed, his antipathy for Zev had shifted into overdrive and he was sure that he would never recover from the hurt he had suffered when his gesture of friendship was repaid with putrid waste.

"I am *not* sending *mishloach manos* to Zev this year!" Yisrael announced repeatedly to his family. The very mention of the approaching holiday generated painful associations for him, and his only catharsis lay in his determination to snub his snobby sibling.

Like every Purim, Avner was the head of his family's *mishloach manos* disbursement, a job aided by the clearly marked address labels affixed to each package. One neatly wrapped box was to be delivered to 51 Rechov Sorotzkin.

Due to an error, a subconscious desire not to travel so far, or the obvious — Providence — Avner knocked on the door of a family on the second floor of *15* Sorotzkin. Somehow the apartment seemed vaguely familiar.

The door opened and Avner Stein froze in his

tracks as an imposing Uncle Zev stared down at him. Avner quickly weighed his options: He could run for it, admit to having made a mistake, or pretend that he needed to use the facilities. But instead he meekly said, "This is for you," and summarily handed over the box. He then tried to beat a hasty retreat but Zev foiled that plan by closing the door and ordering him to wait.

He would not permit his brother to send him another spite package and allow the emissary to get off scot-free. With tremulous fingers, Zev opened up the box and his pupils dilated to their fullest. He examined every item for booby traps, eyed the nervous boy standing at the doorway, and then asked him to wait another minute.

Zev grabbed an enormous shopping bag, filled it with the finest goodies in the house, scribbled a note inside, and handed the sack to his nephew. "Take this home," he instructed, "and feel free to nosh from it along the way."

WHEN AVNER trudged into the house with the elaborate *mishloach manos*, everyone stopped what he was doing to inspect the haul. The shopping bag was practically as tall as he was, and brimming with booty. Wine, grape juice, cherry brandy, banana liqueur, Amaretto, and three cans of beer lined the bottom of the bag. The middle was stuffed with *hamentaschen* and other baked goods galore, while the top was filled with candies as expensive as they were exquisite.

Quite a tidy sum was represented in that *mishloach manos* and the Steins were understandably curious as to who their kind benefactor was. But Avner was speechless. At first they attributed the grand gift to someone who owed them money, or had never returned a borrowed item and was trying to absolve himself with this grand gift, but they could think of no one who owed them *that* much. The speculation soon ceased, however, when the following note was found inside:

Dear Yisrael,

In appreciation. Best wishes for a happy Purim and for the rest of our lives.

Zev

ISRAEL was struck dumb. He read and reread the note and was unquestionably very touched, but one expression in the card put him off: what did his brother mean by "in appreciation"?

He grabbed Avner by the arm and led him out to the porch to interrogate him.

"How did you get this *mishloach manos*?"

Avner fidgeted uncomfortably and attempted a few quickly thought-out excuses, but his father saw right through them. Finally he admitted his error *and* what had happened the previous year.

Yisrael deliberated for a few moments and came to a logical conclusion: If this year's good will was brought about inadvertently, then probably so was all our bad blood. And with this realization, it was indeed a happy Purim for the Stein clan.

Heard from: Rabbi Aaron David

Creature Comfort

ONE MORNING Zeldy, a California housewife, discovered a skunk trapped between her open garage door and the ceiling of the garage. Horrified by the sight of the helpless creature, Zeldy bolted into her house, bolted the door, and bolted down a glass of water to stop herself from hyperventilating.

This was one crisis Zeldy the indoorswoman was determined to resolve immediately. Her first measure was to call the Fire Department. They informed her that they specialized in fires and an occasional cat stuck up a tree, but skunks were outside their domain. She then turned to the ASPCA, which claimed that it was a voluntary organization with a limited number of members, none of whom would be up to this challenge.

With a heavy heart, Zeldy resorted to an extermination company. The exterminators, however, maintained that skunk removal was stinky business and would definitely be an expensive proposition.

"You don't have to kill it," Zeldy pleaded, remembering the *tzaar baalei chaim* interdiction. "As a matter of fact, I wish you wouldn't. It's just trapped. All I want you to do is to free it, so that it can leave my garage on its own."

"Okay, okay," the dispatcher relented at last, "we'll send over our best man."

The anxious housewife counted the seconds. Eventually a van pulled up and out stepped a jumpsuit-attired exterminator brandishing a long, lethal-looking pole. Zeldy closed her eyes and nose, fearing the worst. When at last she dared to look, she found that the van had vanished, as had the exterminator.

STEP BY STEP, inch by inch, Zeldy approached her garage and found the skunk free — and stationary — in the corner near her car. Obviously the exterminator had run for his life when he saw the vindictive varmint poised to release what he knew would be a scent to remember, and be remembered by.

Once again she fled. This time she phoned a rival extermination service and empowered its henchmen to do all that they had to — at any cost — to remove the skunk from her premises.

But as soon as Zeldy hung up, she received a call from the ASPCA informing her that a veteran member of the society was on her way after all to extricate the skunk as humanely as possible.

The frantic housewife called back the extermination company, but its man had just left and he didn't have a two-way radio. Zeldy was in a quandary. It was a race between the forces of good and the forces of evil, both of which were converging on her house at breakneck speed, or at least so she imagined.

A S IT HAPPENED the forces of good arrived a split second before their nemesis, in the person of a feisty septuagenarian wearing baggy dungarees and high tops. Leaping out of her Volkswagen, she rolled up her sleeves and asked, "Now where is that cute little critter?" Zeldy pointed a trembling finger from afar.

In the meantime, the exterminator had arrived and he and the lady who had hired him watched in amazement and dismay as the old lady got down on her knees in the garage and beckoned to the sweet skunk to "come to Auntie Dorothy." Pest controller and *balabusta* stood speechless, anticipating the aroma that might soon engulf them and their environs.

Auntie Dorothy allayed their fears by claiming that she had several pet skunks like this one at home. After some initial hesitation, the skunk calmly ambled its way over to its auntie, who caressed and crooned to her newfound pet. The exterminator waived his fee in exchange for the privilege of witnessing the most mind-boggling sight of his career.

Heard from: Sarah Scheller

Outpatient

IT IS FRIDAY afternoon, eve of the shortest Shabbos of the year, in Jerusalem's Shaare Zedek Medical Center. Outside, there is a flurry of activity as people scurry to hail taxis and pile into the last bus of the day. Inside, the hospital lights are fluorescent, the climate is controlled, and the slow-paced tranquility of the Sabbath schedule has already descended upon the near-empty corridors of this urban medical facility.

Out of the corner of his eye Reb Michel Gutfarb, renowned charity collector and mitzva dispenser, thought he had seen a very famous personage padding down the aisle.

"Can't be," he reasoned to himself, quickening his gait. But just to make sure, he looked again. And yes, there he was. Scarcely an hour before candle lighting, *Hagaon Harav* Shlomo Zalman Auerbach, famed *poseik* and rabbinic giant of our generation, was making his way to the elevator bank.

Their eyes met and Reb Shlomo Zalman rerouted

himself to catch up with Reb Michel. Needless to say, Reb Michel practically galloped over to the venerable sage to spare him the exertion, and reverently inquired what had brought him to the hospital.

Rabbi Auerbach explained that he had come to visit someone two hours earlier, but when he'd seen how lonely the patient was, he felt he could not abandon him after a normal-length visit.

"Since I'm already here," Reb Shlomo Zalman added, "maybe you know of someone else I am acquainted with here whom I could visit?"

Reb Michel glanced quickly at his watch. It was sixty-five minutes before candle lighting, little time for the *gaon* to get home and prepare for Shabbos. On the other hand, someone in the hospital was indeed aching for just such a visit.

AFTER SOME BRIEF DELIBERATION, Reb Michel gently guided Reb Shlomo Zalman along while relating to the sage what had just happened at Shaare Zedek.

"I was walking through one of the wards when I spied a new fellow with a *kipah* on his head. I asked him if he'd had a chance to put on tefillin today, implying that I would be happy to help him if he so desired.

"The fellow contorted his face into a grimace as though he'd just been stabbed in the back. Disgust registered on every contour of his face, indicating that he had entered the cantankerous period of his hospital stay. The man was obviously suffering and

I realized that whatever I would have said or offered would have elicited a similar response.

"'Whom do you think you're talking to?' he muttered at last through clenched teeth. 'Do you take me for an *am ha'aretz?* Do you realize that I attend a weekly *shiur* by Rabbi Shlomo Zalman Auerbach?'

"I apologized, attempting to gratify the infirm man's ego and beat a hasty retreat. I think it would mean a lot to this fellow if the Rav would pay him a brief visit."

REB SHLOMO ZALMAN followed his escort through the wards until they arrived at the room of the injured party. But his bed was empty. The two men looked at each other in perplexity, until a neighboring patient volunteered that the man had just been released.

The two thanked the informant for the update and hastened out of the hospital. As they neared the entranceway Reb Michel offered to call a taxi for the *gaon*, but Reb Shlomo Zalman declined. Instead, he stepped over to a pay phone to glance at the telephone directory.

TWO WEEKS LATER Reb Michel Gutfarb happened to notice that very same ex-patient on a bus. He told him that on that fateful Friday, he'd missed a visit from a very distinguished individual.

"Oh no, I didn't," retorted the man. With obvious

pride he recalled how forty minutes before Shabbos Reb Shlomo Zalman Auerbach, *b' chvodo uv' atsmo,* had arrived at his house to visit him, apologizing profusely that he hadn't managed to catch him in the hospital.

Heard from: Rabbi Michel Gutfarb

Vistas

Raising the Roof

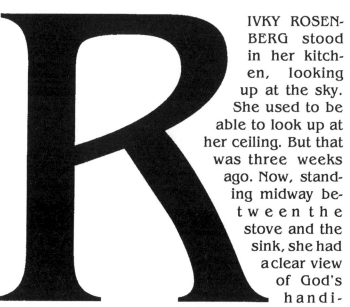

IVKY ROSEN-BERG stood in her kitchen, looking up at the sky. She used to be able to look up at her ceiling. But that was three weeks ago. Now, standing midway between the stove and the sink, she had a clear view of God's handi-work. On bright, sunny days, wispy cirrus clouds, magnificent cumulus clusters, and majestic stratus formations all floated by, casually looking down to sniff what she was cooking.

"I always liked the great outdoors," she would tell her friends. "People pay a lot of money to give their homes a 'natural look.'"

"True, Rivky, but there is still something to be said for having a roof over your head," they would respond.

"It's not as if I don't try. I keep calling the company but all I get is a recording: 'Reliable Roofing — we've got you covered. All our operators are currently busy, but fret not, sweat not. Leave a message at the tone and one of our professional experts will get back to you as soon as — beep.' Mind you, the background Muzak throughout this message is 'Raindrops Keep Falling on My Head.'"

"But Rivky, it's already November! How much longer can you continue to cook outdoors? Once the rainy season begins, your kitchen may suffer from erosion. You'll have flash floods on your floor. And can you imagine a water-logged oven?"

"You don't have to worry. I left the roofer so many messages that I'm sure he'll be back soon. After all, we already gave him $3,000 for the job."

Rivky's friends were skeptical. "This guy not only made a hole in your ceiling, he made a hole in your pocket. You're being awfully naive," they insisted. "It's been weeks already!"

"I guess he's busy," Rivky would shrug her shoulders, "but I seem to be managing. Why, I've devised a whole series of ingenious ways to avoid hypothermia. I use the oven to keep warm, squeeze boots over my thermally encased feet, and zip Nochum's ski parka around my multi-layered torso. Down mittens pad my woolen gloves, and my scarf gets a lot of mileage à la *kaffiyeh*. Aside from the fact that I can hardly move, I feel like I am practically indoors. Admittedly, the birds nesting in my Radar Range are a bit of a nuisance, but if the right gusts prevail they can't vector in for a landing."

Only Rivky Rosenberg could accept her dilemma with such good cheer. If ever someone was born with rose-colored glasses, always affable and never cross, it was she. Life was a madcap adventure for her, and an unpredictable enterprise for those in her company.

NOCHUM ROSENBERG, her lucky match, was the perfect straight man for Rivky's unflappable disposition. A *kollel* fellow with a piercingly analytical mind and a razor-sharp wit, he was also imbued with incredible patience.

In his typical mild manner he asked his young bride, "Why did you choose Reliable Roofing?"

"Do you want to know the truth?" she asked sheepishly.

"Of course I want the truth."

"Naa, you don't really want to know."

"I do, I really do. Why did you pick Reliable Roofing?"

"Because I liked the color of their truck."

"You liked the color of their TRUCK!?"

"I knew you wouldn't want to know. But it was such a pretty shade of blue, with fancy serif lettering emblazoned in gold. Besides, they were $1,500 cheaper than everyone else."

"Didn't you ask for references?"

"Well, no. I mean, yes. Mr. Jones, he's the owner, said that if I wouldn't ask him for any, he wouldn't ask us. Sounded fair to me."

"Seems to me like Jones got the better deal," Nochum commented, just as a scrap of litter wafted in to emphasize the point.

Fortunately the white stuff hadn't begun to fall yet, but the cold, damp wind funnelling into the kitchen indicated that it wasn't far off. It was high time for Nochum to exercise his civic right and take legal action, or at least do something.

"**H**ELLO, SHIA? This is Nochum Rosenberg... That's right, I was two grades below you, but in the same *shiur* when you were a junior... Right, right. I'm sorry to disturb you at home, but I understand you're a lawyer and I need some legal aid.

"We were having our kitchen redone so we hired a roofer. *Reliable* Roofing no less. He took off our roof and then he took off with our money, and we haven't heard from him since. I really need your help to find this Jones guy and get him to fix our roof by the end of this week."

"The end of *this* week?" Shia asked incredulously. "Are you expecting snow or something?"

"No. Worse," Nochum's voice trembled.

"Worse?"

"I'm expecting my mother! She loaned us the money to fix the roof and now she's coming to visit. When she finds out that Rivky and I got taken, she's going to hit the ceiling."

"Assuming you have one by then," the counselor quipped.

"Very funny, but this is no laughing matter. Ever since I became religious ten years ago, my mother has been waiting for me to regret my decision. As far as she is concerned, I could have been a big-time CPA with one house in Scarsdale, another on Cape Cod, and too much business to spend much time in either one. She thinks I'm living like Shimon bar Yochai in the cave, with no friends, no support, and no money."

"Have you ever invited her for Shabbos so that she can see what kind of community you have in Monsey?"

"Of course, but she has no interest. 'That's your thing, not mine' is her favorite disclaimer. And now, out of the blue, she decides to visit."

"Well, she'll see plenty of blue," Shia asserted, but the comment was lost on his former schoolmate. "*Tachlis*, I am dubious if I will be able to locate your unreliable roofer by Friday, but I'll try. If you would like my paralegal counsel, I would recommend that you get your mother to postpone her visit."

Nochum didn't need a lawyer to suggest such

an obvious step. Of course he had tried that, but it was futile. The very hint of the idea brought a fury of indignant accusations raining down upon Nochum's head. And that was nothing compared to what would happen when she got one look at the house.

NOCHUM offered up a heartfelt prayer, and then turned his attention to his wife. "Rivky, let's make this Shabbos extra special. You know how my mother likes everything to be fancy. Let's make everything so posh that she won't even notice the 'outdoor' look. For starters I'll unpack the crystal and you polish the silver."

"With my gloves on?"

"Okay, you unpack the crystal and I'll polish the silver."

"Even unpacking requires more manual dexterity than I think my mummified extremities can handle."

"So what *do* you propose you do for the occasion?"

"You want the house to look like something out of *Better Homes and Gardens*, right?"

"Right."

"Then how about adorning our kitchen with an ice sculpture?"

"Stop! This is serious business."

"You're telling me. She's only your mother, but she's my mother-in-law! Look, why don't we just tell her the truth? Our roof got ripped off, and so did we."

"Don't make jokes."

"I'm not. I'm making Shabbos. And with God's help it will all work out. You'll see."

NOCHUM LOOKED at his wife. Her calm demeanor and complete confidence were therapeutic for his frazzled nerves. "You're right, as usual. But please, I know that around you some-times things just sort of happen. So before they do, promise me they won't. I can't take any more surprises."

"Since when have I given you any surprises?"

"What about the time I walked into the house to find sixteen of your girlfriends gleefully tearing the place apart?"

"Don't exaggerate. It wasn't sixteen of my friends, only fourteen, and I already explained to you that I'd lost my watch. Before nine o'clock I called Sara Susha Pearlman to help me find it and she came right over. My watch's hourly alarm went off on time, but it stopped ringing before we could locate it. Before ten I asked Gitty Klein to join us, and you know Gitty, she was thrilled to help. I was in the kitchen, Sara Susha was in the living room, and Gitty was in the dining room. Well, we heard my watch, but we couldn't find it, so I decided to call out the cavalry for help.

"By ten to eleven, Ellen Sheinberg, Feige Bron-stein, Shiffy Lazarov, Michal Lipshitz, and Chaya

Kraus had arrived. Each friend staked out a different position but how were we to know how elusive a watch could be? It was clear we needed yet a larger posse so we recruited Deena Berger, Chumi Margolis, Bina Lefkowitz, and Judy Stern. Dvory Katz, Doris Ginsberg, and Bluma Shochet saw all the cars parked in front of our house, so they came in, too. It was four seconds to twelve, everyone was poised to strike, and just then you walked in. We weren't about to abandon our search after an hour of anticipation."

"Just a second," Nochum raised his hand in protest. "Your explanation cannot justify what I witnessed. It was like some TV game show — absolute silence, a little beep, and then total pandemonium: grown women ripping pillows off beds, tossing clothes onto the floor, diving into drawers, and hauling up the carpet. Somebody even raided the refrigerator. Suddenly one lady yells, 'I found it,' and everyone screams and shrieks like she's won the lottery!"

Rivky got dreamy-eyed at the recollection. "Maybe I could open a service to locate lost watches that beep. You have to concede that it was spiffy detective work."

"*You* have to concede that it was a scavenger hunt! Rivky," an exasperated Nochum softened his tone, "I could quote two dozen escapades of yours that you also think were exceedingly brilliant. This Shabbos I don't want any brilliance, team efforts, furniture rearranging, or innovative techniques. Just a plain, ordinary, inspiring Shabbos, okay?"

"Okay."

FOR THE NEXT two days, the Rosenbergs scoured their cookbooks to plan a menu only a mother-in-law could love. They ruminated over roulade, boned up on boneless chicken, and took a gander at goose, but nothing seemed quite right. They even ruled out Flounder Florentine ("Maybe that's what we should make. After all, her name is Florence.").

Eventually the two connoisseurs hit upon la recipe that was sure to titillate Mrs. Rosenberg senior's tastebuds: "Chicken à la Français." Nochum assisted in the production by reading out the recipe: "Cut up fryers. Mix flour, salt, and pepper and dredge the chicken... Dredge the chicken? Are you sure that's legal in this state?"

"That means coat the chicken. Now just keep reading."

"Combine oil and margarine. Heat. Brown chicken till it's half-cooked. Layer chopped onion in a Dutch oven. Dutch oven? What is it, powered by a windmill?... Okay, all right, I'll keep on reading.

"Sprinkle oil-margarine on top. Lay chicken on onions. Cover with tomatoes, garlic, and herbs. Baste with one cup of cooking wine and bake at 400° for thirty minutes. Garnish with mushrooms and heat on range for fifteen minutes. Serve over ice — well, we have plenty of that!"

"That's rice! What do you think?"

"I like it. Especially the part about the wine.

Maybe we can get my mother so soused, she won't notice that our kitchen roof is missing."

"Stop worrying. I'm sure your old friend Shia will come up with this guy somehow."

"I'm afraid it's too late. Tomorrow's Friday and my mom's flight is due in at noon. There's no way we're going to have a roof by then."

"Well, maybe we'll have a good excuse instead."

COME FRIDAY MORNING, Nochum braced himself for the big day. He scraped the frost off the kitchen counter, checked the polished silverware, ran his finger along any surface where dust could collect, set the table, and made sure Rivky's watch was safe and sound. The time had come to head off to the airport in a car borrowed from his neighbor and he gave his wife last-minute instructions: "The house is immaculate. All you have to do is make the chicken and come up with a good reason why we don't have a roof over our kitchen."

"No problem. I'm sure *Hashem* will help us think of something. Either that or nature will run its course."

"Nature?"

"You know, nature abhors a vacuum."

"You're right! We should have shampooed the rug!"

"Nochum, relax," Rivky soothed her panic-stricken husband. "Everything will be fine."

Newly amazed at his wife's cockeyed optimism, Nochum set off, leaving Rivky alone with her thoughts and her fryers. She tried furiously to fasten her apron around her husband's ski parka but the straps weren't long enough to circumnavigate her winter gear circumference. Undaunted, she picked up a *pulka* and picked up the phone.

"Gitty? Hi! Just peeling potatoes and cleaning chickens. My mother-in-law's coming and I'm trying to make something nice. Let me tell you, it's not easy trying to cook without a roof. Every twenty minutes, I have to take a break and let my fingers thaw. I could become an entrepreneur and market frozen food!"

BY THE EARLY AFTERNOON Rivky's Shabbos preparations were beginning to take shape. After only six phone calls, the chickens were ready and the cholent was on the fire. She was just beginning to cut up the salads when the phone rang.

"Hello! Rivky's Catering Service. You ring, we bring. Shabbos is our specialty."

"Uhhhh," a whiny sing-song of a voice began to speak. Midway through his first sentence Rivky knew who it was. And worse, she knew what it meant. "This is Mr. Weingeroff."

"Oh, shreck-and-a-half!" Rivky thought angrily. "How come he always calls at the wrong time? I still have to make a bunch of desserts!"

"Yes, Mr. Weingeroff. A *gutten erev Shabbos!*"

She forced herself to be more jovial than she felt. "What can I do for you?"

"Do you have any Shabbos food to spare?" he began, his tone achieving all the modulation of a car that won't start. "I can't get to the market. My daughter doesn't make anything I like. I've called the Jewish Family Service, the JCC, and that other group, whatever their name is, but nobody has anything for me. They all want me to drop dead, or worse, to starve to death."

"That's not true. I'm sure they all love you and care for you and want to help you. In fact, I called your social worker just last week and she told me that you were fully capable of taking care of yourself."

"What does she know?" he sniffed with self-pity. "Does she have my aches and pains? Does she have my nervous stomach? All she knows is that I'm alive, no thanks to her. I practically died of malnourishment this week."

"Didn't she arrange for you to go shopping?"

"Arrange for me to go?! You mean like tell me that the supermarket is open from nine until nine? Even that she would consider major assistance. Besides, I can't go by myself. I'm too weak to push the shopping carts, and too tired to stand in line. I need help or I'm done for. What have you got for Shabbos?"

"Chicken à la Français, Yerushalmi kugel, sweet potato cholent, fluffed rice meringue, cucumber vinaigrette, eggplant dip, chocolate pudding whip and..."

"You can stop, that's enough."

"I'm sorry, Mr. Weingeroff, but I can't. I just can't. My mother-in-law is coming and I don't have enough food to spare."

"What's more important, my life or your mother-in-law's culinary appreciation?"

"Mr. Weingeroff, what did you eat last night?"

"Cat food."

"Cat food?" Rivky gasped with sudden alarm.

"You call it tuna fish. I call it cat food."

"I see. And the night before that?"

"I don't remember. It was either very old meat or very new cheese."

"What about the night before that?"

"I'm not sure. I think I chewed on my belt until I fell asleep."

"All right, all right. As usual, you win. I'll bring over a little something in a few minutes."

"Make it a lot of something, and right now, and we got a deal."

"Mr. Weingeroff!"

"Bless you, Mrs. Rottenberg."

"It's Rosenberg!"

"That's what I said. You're an angel from Heaven."

"Good gravy!" Rivky said to herself. "How do I get myself into these things?"

RIVKY PUT TOGETHER a modest care package. "At least I don't have to put my coat on to go outside!" she chuckled.

Ten minutes later, Rivky arrived at chez Weingeroff. Ever since his wife passed away seven months ago, Mr. Weingeroff had not so much as lifted a finger around the house. Heavy curtains shrouded the windows. The doors were bolted. Grass grew tall and unkept on what used to be a nice lawn. An outsider might have assumed that the house had been abandoned, and he wouldn't have been far off.

Rivky rang the doorbell. There was no answer.

"Hello? Mr. Weingeroff? It's Rivky Rosenberg! I have your Shabbos food."

One of the curtains began to move. This was followed by the front door slowly creaking open and a slight, balding, sad-eyed man peeking out from behind the crack in the doorway.

"What took you so long? I almost starved to death. I was sure I wouldn't last until you came."

"Well, I'm glad to see you're still around. Where can I put this?"

"The chicken I'll eat now. The rest, put in the icebox."

"What about Shabbos? Shouldn't you save the chicken for Shabbos?"

"I feel weak. If I don't eat something now, I won't make it till then!"

"What a con!" Rivky thought to herself as she

began unpacking a leg of chicken, a bowl of rice, and a pot of cholent. She placed the chicken on a semi-clean plate and served it to the ailing man slumped over the kitchen table. For such a frail individual, Mr. Weingeroff certainly attacked the bird with gusto.

RIVKY OPENED the refrigerator, expecting to find it well-stocked with other care packages, fast foods, and groceries. But the fridge was completely bare except for a dim light bulb that shined bleakly on its dirty, once-white walls.

Rivky opened the cabinets over the counters. Nothing. Then she opened the cabinets under the counters. Also nothing.

"What are you looking for? I don't have any money."

"I'm not looking for money. I'm looking for food."

"I don't have any of that, either, if that's what you're doing here. If you're hungry, try someplace else."

"Mr. Weingeroff, you really were starving? You weren't kidding?"

"A dying man has no time for jokes."

"I'm so sorry! Forgive me, please. I'm going home to get you more food. I'll be right back. Meanwhile, try the rice — you'll love it!"

"Thank you. You're being very kind. I appreciate it."

RIVKY DROVE HOME in tears. The sight of a completely empty kitchen just ten minutes away from her home filled her heart with compassion. She ran to her cupboards and stuffed two large boxes full of food.

In the first one she inserted everything she had prepared for Shabbos, from soup to nuts. The second box she crammed with items she pulled down from the pantry: cereal, pasta, preserves, beans, olives, felafel mix, matzo meal, salt — anything she imagined Mr. Weingeroff could use. Afterwards she tithed her refrigerator of all its fruits and vegetables. Struggling to keep her balance, she shlepped the bursting boxes out to her car and drove off.

Mr. Weingeroff was uncharacteristically appreciative. "Mrs. Rottenberg, I don't know how to thank you. My life is almost worth living."

"Don't thank me, Mr. Weingeroff. I'm happy to help. And I'll call your social worker after Shabbos. And when I do, you can be sure I'll tell her what I saw!"

RIVKY ROSENBERG drove home with the heady feeling of having spared a fellow Jew from starvation. But when she stepped back into her kitchen, the glamor of her rescue was abruptly shattered by reality. A sense of impending disaster zeroed in — she had given away her entire Shabbos!

Rivky searched frantically for something to make but all she found were some cans of tomato soup and a bag of rice cakes. In just half an hour Nochum would be back with his never-needing-an-excuse-to-find-fault mother...

NOCHUM ROSENBERG spotted his mother in LaGuardia Airport right away. The paucity of women swaggering around looking totally disgusted and weighing in conservatively at 250 pounds certainly narrowed it down.

"Mom! I'm over here."

"It's about time you showed up!" Mrs. Rosenberg barked, decidedly underwhelmed at seeing her son after so long.

"The traffic in from Monsey was horrible. But I made it. And *Baruch Hashem*, I'm glad you did, too."

"Don't give me any of your 'BaruSams.' I was just about to turn around and go home. Why did you have to pick Monsey? You couldn't find what you were looking for in Durham? We got temples, too, you know."

"Look, Ma, I've told you a hundred times already, Monsey is a very close community. The *ches*, er, kindness there is amazing. We're very happy there; people like us and we like them."

"We shall see."

"You will. In the meantime, since this is your first Shabbos with us, let me tell you all the wonderful things Rivky's made in your honor..."

Nochum regaled his mother with a foretaste of Rivky's gastronomic prestidigitation. He went over each and every recipe in mouthwatering detail, adding as many adjectives as he could to help make the overall impression even more appealing...

"And the Chicken à la Français? Wait till you taste it! Baby mushrooms handpicked for flavor, tender chicken bathed in wine sauce and nestled on a bed of fresh garden herbs — it's positively out of this world!"

"Sounds good," Florence Rosenberg said in spite of herself. "I may even end up enjoying this Shabbos after all."

"We sure hope so. There's just one thing I've got to tell you. It's about our roof..."

Mrs. Rosenberg suddenly became animated. "I hope you found someone else to do the job in the end. $3,000 to fix a kitchen roof! That's highway robbery! It's totally outrageous! It wouldn't cost half that in Durham. If I saw that roofer of yours, I'd give him a piece of my mind."

"So would I!" Nochum thought. His mother kept complaining about the price and he continued to try and change the subject by describing all the delicacies in store. By the time Nochum finished his marathon filibuster about Rivky's epicurean tour de force, they were finally in Monsey. "I know you're going to feel just as much at home here as we do," Nochum boasted, just as a few black-clad *chassidim* passed in front of the car and a tidal wave of nausea passed over Florence Rosenberg.

SHLEPPING her heavy suitcase in one hand and holding the front door open with the other, Nochum led his mother into his ventilated abode. She wasn't more than two steps into the house when she commented, "Hmm... that smells like tomato soup. I hate tomato soup! There's also a terrible draft in this house."

"Eh, I... I'll go check." In a second Nochum had scurried into the kitchen and quickly sealed the door behind him.

"Hi," Rivky said nervously. "Don't tell me, your mother's not hungry."

"Rivky, are you making tomato soup?"

"Yes and no. It's a special recipe — homespun, I might add — that calls for a little tomato soup."

"A *little*?" Nochum gasped.

"Okay, in this particular case, considering the dearth of other ingredients, I guess it is a little of a lot... But regardless, it's really some dish. The ingredients enter into a mysterious synergy, a relationship marked not by overlapping interests but by mutual respect. In other words, they don't step all over one another, but stand out in glorious relief. I call it 'Rice Cakes Italiano.'"

"Rice Cakes Italiano?! What happened to the Chicken à la Français?"

"Well, er... you got the right continent, but the wrong state of affairs. You see, I've decided that we should eat more healthfully. You know, less meat, more whole grains. And accordingly, the Chicken à la Français went thata way," she said, pointing simultaneously to the front door and the hole over the kitchen. "Olé!"

"Rivky," Nochum seethed, "where's the chicken?"

"Uh... I gave it away."

"You gave it away?!" Nochum screamed. "And the rest of our Shabbos?"

"Nochum, please don't be upset. But I gave that away, too. It was a mitzva! Honest. You know how hard I..."

Mrs. Rosenberg swung open the kitchen door. "Hi, Mom," Rivky waved, but her mother-in-law was too busy sniffing to reciprocate. Eventually she hooked onto a waft and followed her nose until it pointed to the... sky!

"Nakoom!" she bellowed. "Where is your roof? Who stole your roof? I gave you three thousand dollars to fix your roof. Now where is it?"

"Ding dong!" went the chimes of the front door. "Saved by the bell," Nochum sighed. "Ma, I can explain everything; just wait until I get the door."

BUT NOBODY WAITED. Nochum, his mother, and Rivky all ran to the front door, two of the three hoping to forestall the greatest tripartite conflict since the Normandy Invasion.

Nochum opened the door and came face to face with a man in a body cast from his calf up, teetering over a pair of crutches and massaging his bandaged cranium with taped-together fingers.

"What the... Mr. Jones? Is that you?"

"I'm not sure, but I think so," an embarrassed

voice responded. "May we come in?"

"Please do."

"Mr. Jones wants to apologize for not calling you," said Shia Lieberman, Esq. "I found him flat on his back at Tri-County Hospital, staring at the ceiling, of all things. No one answered your phone, so I assumed it was out of order. Anyway, the hospital gave me permission to take him out for a while. Mr. Jones would like to tell you what happened so he won't be arrested for theft. Right, Mr. Jones?"

"Yeah, right. You see, I had this other client. I guess I got careless. Anyway, I fell two stories. But they managed to put Humpty Dumpty back together again."

"But why didn't you call us?"

"When you didn't hear from me, I figured you'd get someone else."

"And my money?"

"Well, like I was tellin' the lawyer here, I was plannin' to return it as soon as I got out of the hospital. But if you'd prefer, maybe I could have my brother-in-law finish the job for you — he's also a roofer, although he doesn't have my sense of balance."

"I see. Well, let's talk about that after —"

"Ding dong." All eyes turned to the front door.

"Can we come in?"

"Only if you have your coats on," Mrs. Rosenberg said drily.

IN MARCHED Sara Susha Pearlman, Gitty Klein, and Ellen Sheinberg, each bearing steaming trays of food. "Gitty told me you were trying to cook a special Shabbos for your mother-in-law," began Sara, and as if on cue all three smiled at Mrs. Rosenberg, "so we wanted to help."

"Welcome to Monsey, Mrs. Rosenberg," Gitty said warmly. "We want you to feel as much at home here as Nochum and Rivky do!"

"Why, thank you," Mrs. Rosenberg said, enjoying the attention and especially the aroma of the edibles.

"Ding ,dong!" Again, the crowded assemblage turned toward the door.

Feige Bronstein, Chaya Kraus, Shiffy Lazarov, Michal Lipshitz, and Deena Berger were standing on the steps. Feige held a large bouquet of flowers, Chaya was balancing a chocolate cake with thick icing, Shiffy was hefting three bottles of fine wine, Michal cradled two different bowls of salad, and Deena displayed an enormous, homemade *challah*.

"May we come in?"

Florence Rosenberg welcomed them with open arms.

"When Gitty told us what was going on," Deena gushed, "we all wanted to share in the mitzva."

The conversation was about to revert to Jones' alibi, with the ladies in the background setting the table and arranging things up in the kitchen, when the doorbell rang yet again.

On the porch were Judy Stern and Dvory Katz. "When we saw all the cars parked outside," they explained, "we wanted to know what was going on. It's *erev Shabbos*, but we always have time to look for a watch."

MRS. ROSENBERG looked at Shia Lieberman, who looked at Mr. Jones, who looked only where his neckbrace allowed. Nochum simply rolled his eyes.

"We want to make sure Mrs. Rosenberg feels at home here," Feige said, offering everyone a drink.

"Well, Ma, how do you feel?"

MRS. ROSENBERG looked at the horde of women mulling about her son's house and then broke into her first smile since Nochum had become religious. "This, you don't have in Durham."

Rivky hugged her mother-in-law, to the delight of all the bystanders, when the doorbell rang again. An official-looking woman whom no one recognized stood outside, clutching a clipboard. "Does Mrs. Rottenberg live here? I am Mr. Max Weingeroff's social worker..."

Heard from: Mrs. Perie Hirshaut

Not So Long Ago
And Not So Far Away

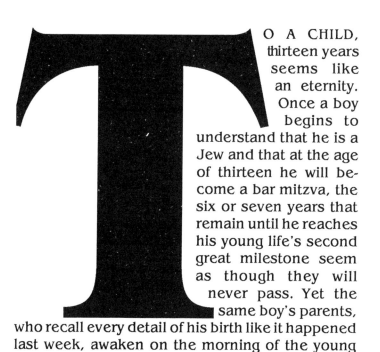

TO A CHILD, thirteen years seems like an eternity. Once a boy begins to understand that he is a Jew and that at the age of thirteen he will become a bar mitzva, the six or seven years that remain until he reaches his young life's second great milestone seem as though they will never pass. Yet the same boy's parents, who recall every detail of his birth like it happened last week, awaken on the morning of the young man's entry into adulthood and wonder if the last thirteen years have been a dream.

For a parent, particularly a mother, every aspect of a child's birth is indelibly etched upon her mind. For the child, however, unless the events that surround his birth are brought home in some unusually cogent manner, they are dismissed as prehistory. No matter how many times he hears about how Mommy said it was time, how Daddy called the ambulance, and how they laughed when they first saw him because he was all purple, and his eyes were crossed, and he didn't have any hair, etc., etc., etc., for him, it remains the story of someone with whom he is but vaguely familiar.

THIS IS THE STORY of thirteen years and a birth so unusual that for a handful of people, who were not even blood relations, every detail remains to this day vivid and unforgettable. The birth was unusual not in the clinical sense, but in the historical sense — unusual in that which preceded and followed it.

It is the story of Menasheleh, growing up under what seemed to him to be perfectly normal conditions. For him, his entrance into the world and into our people's immortal Covenant remained more or less a mystery, over which he had never lost much sleep.

But mostly it is the story of the saintly Leah, Menasheleh's mother.

Leah had always been able to keep a secret. That's why on her wedding day, her father shared with her his own greatest secret: "Leah'leh," he began, "I have something I wish to reveal to you. I want it to remain a secret, at least during my lifetime, but someone else should know it, and I know that you, Leah, although you are only seventeen years old, will understand why. A number of years ago, after I had begun writing my *sefer* on the Maharsha, I saw him. I saw the *heiligeh* Maharsha in a dream. He came to me and thanked me. He told me that my work would help countless *lamdanim* understand his *perush* better. He told me that it was essential that I continue my work, and then he kissed me!"

For many years after her father's death, Leah did not reveal his secret to a living soul. But her father was right, she had understood it. She had understood it very well, and shortly after her wedding, she sold all her jewelry — that is, everything of value that she owned — to finance the publication of her father's *sefer*.

BUT THERE WAS, after all, nothing secret about the events surrounding the birth of Menasheleh, whom Leah had named for her missing husband's father. Nevertheless, Leah was one to hold her peace. It would never have occurred to her to boast, and besides, for the holiest and saintliest members of our people, *mesirus nefesh* hardly seems remarkable. Neither does God's guiding hand.

Thus, when Leah was miraculously reunited with her husband, the learned Reb Yitzchak Zev, and when she and her family made it to the land of the free and the home of the brave, she did not immediately contact some literary agent to help her negotiate the rights to her wartime memoirs.

Nor did she seek out a screenwriter to sell and tell her astounding story to the "enlightened" world. Instead, settling in Sommerville, New Jersey, and subsequently in Williamsburg, Brooklyn, she dedicated herself to the fulfillment of the secret vow she had made during some of the darkest days our People have ever known. Only after her death did her husband find a yellowed slip of paper containing a short note, written in Hebrew, which she had dated 12 Menachem Av, 5704 (1944):

> I have been here for three weeks. My husband, father, family, and *klal Yisrael* are in exile, I know not where, and I have heard nothing of them. Here in this camp, at three o'clock in the afternoon, I hereby make a *neder* that if *HaKadosh Baruch Hu* reunites me with my family and with *klal Yisrael* I will bring up my children to be dedicated to *Yiddishkeit*, and I will help them and their father learn Your Torah all their days.

And she did.

She, her family, and her husband's yeshiva settled first in Sommerville, remaining there for just one year before moving to Mt. Kisco, New York. When the children became older and needed to attend school, the family relocated to

Williamsburg, but the yeshiva remained in Mt. Kisco. Leah's husband, who was a *rosh yeshiva*, had little choice but to commute between Mt. Kisco and Williamsburg, leaving Leah and the children alone from Sunday through Thursday. Five days out of seven, Leah was father and mother, maid, cook, administrator, confidante, nurse, psychologist, educator, and role model to her children. But she did not mind. In fact, during this time, she also gave *shiurim* to women, excelled in *bikur cholim* and other acts of *chessed*, and established a women's organization for the support of Torah institutions. Despite all of her accomplishments, she hardly thought herself extraordinary. For Torah is the life of the Jew, and where Torah is concerned, there are no limits to self-sacrifice.

Leah even found time to celebrate, and thirteen years after Menasheleh was born, in a place from which so many had not returned, it was time to make a *bris*. A *bris*?! Yes, *morai ve-rabbosai*, a *bris*. For Menasheleh. But don't worry. It was not his first.

HAVE YOU EVER been to a bar mitzva in Williamsburg? I mean old Williamsburg, ten or fifteen extremely short years after the liberation of Europe. Who better than the Jewish residents of Williamsburg knew how few had returned from the European inferno? And who better understood the meaning of a bris, bar mitzva, or wedding?

A Williamsburg bar mitzva. The surroundings,

and even the fashions, may have been modest. The food was not. Do you like your gefilte fish sweet or spicy? Why choose? Have a little of each. Or why not a lot? How many kinds of herring can you imagine? Double that number and add five. Think of rafts of every type of kugel known to mankind, cut into perfect squares. Think of steaming cholent measured not in pots but in washtubs, kishke sliced not by the pound but by the mile, and tzimmes made from enough carrots to feed every rabbit on the eastern seaboard for a month. Think of armies of soda bottles, brigades of schnapps, and platoons of beer bottles. And marvel at the scores of cows and chickens that made the supreme sacrifice to participate in the celebration of Menasheleh's bar mitzva.

Imagine a cacophony of loud, ebullient Yiddish, mostly spoken with a Hungarian dialect. Picture rows of tables covered with white tablecloths and adorned with dishes, glasses, and cutlery — all purely utilitarian but spotlessly clean. Picture two rooms, a bit overdue for a paint job, adjoined by a door and perhaps a small window. Picture one room filled with black coats and long beards and the other filled with long skirts, long sleeves, and *tichelach*.

PICTURE MENASHELEH, with a slight downy growth about his upper lip and chin, looking just a bit bewildered in his ill-fitting first hat and *kapota*, sitting at the head table next to his *rosh yeshiva* father. Picture his father with more gray hair and wrinkles than a man his age should have, but looking self-assured and grateful. Picture him quietly accepting *mazel tovs* while his wife, whose cheeks had reclaimed their rosy hue, and whose once-emaciated frame had regained its humanity, sneaks doting glances at the young apple of her eye.

And picture one more guest. A man. A bit shabbier than the rest, a bit more bent over. At the table, two vacant chairs separate him from the nearest celebrant. His salt-and-pepper beard is unkempt even by Williamsburg standards, and his mangy *shtreimel* reminds one of the theoretical possibility of substance without form. The sleeves of his *kapota* are frayed, and his shiny pants are a mite too short. He speaks with no one and hardly touches his food. His hands exhibit a slight tremor, but his eyes, his amazingly green eyes, *rabbosai*, shine like two emeralds.

No one seems to recognize this strange figure. Yet no one is terribly concerned about his presence – if an indigent has snuck in from the street, *nu*, there's not enough food to go around? Even Leah, if she has seen him, has no idea who he is, even though she once knew him well.

EVENTUALLY THE STEAMING PLATTERS cease their restless shuttling back and forth from table to table. The muted rattle of knives and forks against plates dies down. The rav gives his *derashah* and before the father of the bar mitzva is to give his, it is young Menasheleh's turn to present his laboriously studied *pilpul*. As he stands and clears his throat, so does another figure, one with green eyes, who seems oblivious to the events transpiring at the head table. At the sound of his loud, raspy "ahem," all heads turn in his direction. Those quicker on the uptake are already shouting "*shah*" in a typically Williamsburgian stage whisper and none-too-subtly motioning for the interloper to sit down. One fast-thinking, enterprising guest pushes a bottle of schnappes towards the man; another a plate of kugel. But the stranger's emerald eyes, as if chipped from agate, are fixed upon Menasheleh, who is by now quite at a loss as to whether to remain standing or take his seat.

As if no one has yet noticed him, the stranger picks up a bottle of soda and, in the time-honored tradition of Jewish gatherings, begins clinking his spoon against its side, calling for quiet and attention. The hand motions and shouts of "*shah*" are coming from all quarters now, and men are beginning to whisper all sorts of speculations concerning the identity of this nuisance.

But the man is undaunted. This is without a doubt the loudest and most persistent soda-bottle clinker in the history of New York *simchas*. With little choice, Menasheh's father touches the boy's shoulder, quietly signaling him to be seated, and raises his hand patiently for silence so that the uninvited eccentric can have his hearing.

The room quickly hushes, and the figure, in a voice of surprising strength and clarity, calls out one word: "Menasheleh." The boy fixes a wide-eyed stare upon the man, and the voice is heard again, but this time it is an octave or so higher, and it is singing. It is singing that tune so familiar to anyone who has studied in yeshiva and so unknown to the rest of the world. It is the tune that non-religious Jews hear perhaps once a year — when the Four Questions are asked at the *seder.* This time, this yeshiva sing-song has just one word: "Menasheleh." And then, after a shorter pause, still in sing-song, "Menasheleh, *oy mein* Menasheleh."

And the song continues: "*Rabboisai, moirai ve-rabboisai.* You think this kugel is *geshmak*? Have I got news for you! I once tasted kugel many times better!" All the while singing: "*Moirai ve-rabboisai,* you think we're here to celebrate Menasheleh's bar mitzva? Well, I've got even bigger news for you! We're here to celebrate Menasheleh's *bris.*"

By now many of the guests are feeling quite indignant. First, this vagabond insults the food, and then he insults the... On the other hand, the hook is in, and everybody realizes that there is much more here than meets the eye. And so the stranger, feeling that he has his audience in the palm of his grizzled hand, continues his song: "A story, *rabboisai*; listen to a story. It happened not so long ago, and not so far away.

"**I**T WAS already the summer of 1944. The Nazis, *yemach shemam ve-zichram,* were in a hurry. Their enemies were closing in fast. But by this time, *rabboisai,* half of Hungary's Jews were ashes. We did not know this, of course, but when they put us on that train, very few of us thought we'd ever come back.

"How many *heiligeh, chusheveh Yiddin* died on

that train, *rabboisai*, don't ask. None of us ever counted. How many lost their minds? Who knows. But when we got there... when we got there, the first thing they did was throw out the bodies. The doors to that freight car opened wide, *rabboisai*, and before our eyes had even recovered from the sudden flash of sunlight, we could hear the thud of bodies hitting the pavement. It was fresh asphalt, and later, when they made us lug the bodies away from the train, most of them had stuck, *Rachmana litzlan*.

"But, you will ask, where were we? Believe it or not, *rabboisai*, we were in Vienna. Ah, Vienna. But believe me, *rabboisai*, we were not there to waltz or gaze at the Danube. Later, after the war, we found out that the Nazis made short work of generations of Jewish life in Hungary. We found out that every train loaded with Hungary's Jews went straight to Auschwitz. Every train except for five. About one of these trains, I would not like to talk, *rabboisai*; some things are better left unsaid. It is about the other four, I want to tell you.

"**F**OUR TRAINS, *rabboisai*, four trains, filled with precious, *heiligeh Yiddin*. Why? Only the *Aibishter* knows, *rabboisai*, that's for certain. The *Aibishter* is the only One who will ever know. After the war, I tried to find out. Don't think I didn't. I asked everyone. Anyone who would listen. I was crazy," he begins to whisper as the sing-song fades. "I had to know why my train went to Vienna when all of Hungary's *Yiddin* went to the furnaces of Auschwitz. Finally I got to some professor. A former Jew, but don't get me wrong, *rabboisai*, a very nice man. He writes books, history; makes a living off the Second World War. But a very nice man all the same.

"He sits me down and makes me a cup of tea. I don't drink it, of course, but very nice. He asks me if he can turn on his tape recorder. 'Why not?' I say. He turns on his tape recorder and asks me about 'my wartime experiences.' I tell him my English it's not so good. He tells me I can answer in Yiddish. He's got a nice boy from Brooklyn translates for him.

"After about an hour of asking me questions, he answers mine. 'We don't know,' he says. 'We just don't know. It's too early to tell. It will take generations to comb through all of the Nazi archives. There are thousands, maybe millions of papers. Most of them are in Israel,' he tells me. 'That's where most of the research is going on, and that's where most of the survivors are. But it may be a hundred years before all those documents have been analyzed. And who knows if they will shed any light on those four trains? Yes, I know of those four trains. It's an interesting problem.'

"'An interesting problem?!' I think to myself.

"'I could write a paper on that, I certainly could,' he says, looking at the wall.

"'What does this mean, a paper?' I ask.

"'Oh, nothing, nothing at all,' he says, looking back at me. 'Anyway, those four trains are an interesting problem. One I've thought about myself. Look here, Mr. uh...'

"'Call me Yisruel.'

"'Yes, Mr. Yisruel. The best we can figure...'

"'Who is this "we"?' I keep asking myself.

"'...is that by that stage of the hostilities, there was no slave labor remaining in Vienna.'

"'What does this word mean, "hostilities"?'

"'Hostilities means the war. The war. Anyway, by this stage of the war, the mayor of Vienna may have appealed to the SS for help. By that time, many of the slaves may have died in the bombardments; many more had probably died of starvation and disease. There was plenty of work. The Allied bombers had left the city in shambles, and tremendous manpower was required just to keep the streets clear. There are records of other such arrangements. The mayor would have had to pay the SS a fee for transporting and maintaining you. Out of that fee, the SS would have paid for your food and clothing, etc.'

"'What food?! What clothing?!' I shout.

"'Yes, I understand,' he tells me. 'Be that as it may, the city of Vienna would have transferred funds from its budget to that of the SS. The more economically the SS ran its operation, the more it would have profited from the service it provided. The SS officers may even have skimmed some off the top.'

"'What does this mean, "economically," and "skimmed some off the top"?' I ask, and I see his former Jewish eyes fill up. He can't answer me right away. Like I said, he's a nice man. Then he says, 'They tried to save money on your food.' He clears his throat.

"'But we don't know yet.' Again we. 'We do know that the camp where you were taken, Strasshof, was a transfer camp for slave labor.' This he knows without me telling him. 'And we know that until you arrived, there had never been any Jews there. It was manned by Germans and Ukrainians...' He knows his concentration camps, this professor. 'But you're right, Mr. uh... How do you pronounce that again?'

"'Yisruel.'

"'Ah, yes, Yisruel, thank you. It was very strange, those four trains. Very strange indeed, Mr. Yisruel.'

"'Thanks a lot, Professor Knows-Only-Facts,' I'm thinking. '*You* I need to tell me that it's strange? *You* I need to tell me about the Ukes with their clubs? *You* I need to tell me about the beatings and the starvation? *You* I need to tell me how everyone above the age of nine worked a minimum of thirteen hours a day? How they had little children shlepping debris from bombed out buildings? *You* I need to tell me how many *heiligeh Yiddin* died there? *Nu, nu*, it could have been worse. At least the Austrians didn't throw us out of the shelters when the bombers came. At least they slipped us food sometimes, on the sly. Compared to the rest of the Jews of Europe, we were in a country club! But why us? Why these four trains?'

"But like I said, he's a nice man, so instead of shouting, I say to him, 'Thank you very much, Herr

Professor. Thank you for your time.'

"And he says to me, 'But you didn't even touch your tea.'

"'It's okay,' I tell him. 'I wasn't thirsty.'

"**F**OUR TRAINS, *rabboisai*," the sing-song resumes. "Four trains, and on one of them a woman who's expecting. A woman, I said? She's really no more than a *maideleh*. Where's her husband? She doesn't know. Isn't she afraid to give birth? No, no. She already has two daughters; giving birth doesn't scare her, but something else does. What if it's a boy? How will she make a *bris*? *Rabboisai*, have you ever heard of a devout woman with two daughters pray for a girl?! But that's what she does. Better a girl than a boy without a *milah*. But she brings one clean diaper with her, so that if it is a boy, he will have a nice, clean diaper for his *bris*.

"Some would call it *mazel, rabboisai*; others would call it *Hashgacha*. No matter. This woman, her name is Leah, gets an 'easy' job working in an office because she speaks so many languages. This is Tammuz, she's due in Tishrei, and all the time she's praying for a girl and trading rations for cigarettes. Why cigarettes, Leah'leh? You don't smoke? Ah but this we all know, don't we, *rabboisai*? We all know that cigarettes were the currency of the camps. What will be when the baby is born, if she needs to buy something for him? If she needs some special favor? So all the time she's trading rations for cigarettes. Thank God, it's an easy pregnancy; at least she's not shlepping heavy loads and getting beaten every day.

"She's such a wonderful woman, always doing favors, always encouraging everyone, and a wonderful mother to her own little girls. They're too young to work. All day they're alone. 'If the bombers come,' she tells them, 'run into the woods. They don't drop bombs in the woods.' But at night, when she comes home to them, she sings to them, and tells them stories to strengthen their *emunah*. One of them gets sick, *Rachmana litzlan*. The child never comes back.

"Anyway, everybody loves our Leah'leh, and everybody wants to help. And all the time, she's praying for a girl and trading rations for cigarettes.

" **B**UT THE *AIBISHTER*, He plays a trick. First He sends our Leah'leh to Vienna instead of Auschwitz, then He gets her a 'good' job in an office, and then what does He do, *rabboisai*? A *broch*! He gives her a boy!

"'What will be?' she wonders. The day after the birth, she's already on her feet. She's talking to Dr. Tuchman. Tuchman wasn't a *tzaddik*, but even within a *Judenraat*-encased heart there is still a spark of a *Yiddisheh neshamah*. Sometimes he's willing to help his fellow *Yiddin*. 'Dr. Tuchman,' she tells him, 'I want you should get me permission from the *lagerfuehrer* to make a *bris*.'

"'Young woman,' he tells her, 'what's the matter with you!? Amalek should give permission to have a *bris*? They're already asking when you'll be back at work. I don't even want to mention your name!

Go hide and nurse your baby, and I'll try to get you as many days off as I can.'

"'But Dr. Tuchman,' she says, 'a boy must have a *bris* on his eighth day. It says so in the Torah!' She's a learned woman, this Leah'leh.

"'But, young woman...'

"**B**UT LEAH'LEH, she doesn't know from 'buts.' 'Dear Dr. Tuchman, when *Hashem* gave us the mitzva of *milah*, He didn't say that we're exempted in a concentration camp. We still have to keep His *mitzvos*. If He decides that I can't make a *bris*, then I won't be able to make a *bris*. But until I know otherwise, I have no choice but to try. So if you won't speak to the *lagerfuehrer*, I'll do it myself.'

"*Nu, rabboisai*, how do you say no to such a *tzaddekes*? Even Tuchman couldn't.

"And so the next day, he's there bright and early. 'Young woman, I can't believe it. I spoke with Amalek himself, and he says you can make a *bris*! You must have had quite a father to earn this *zechus*!'

"But Leah'leh doesn't smile. She's got another worry on her mind. 'Who will be the *mohel*?' she asks.

"'Why, my dear, I'll do it myself,' says Tuchman. After all, he's an M.D.

"But Leah'leh looks away. 'Maybe I shouldn't make a *bris*. The baby seems so weak...'

"Tuchman looks at her for a minute like this time she's really *meshugeh*. 'Cancel the *bris* after Amalek himself has agreed?!' But then he understands. 'All right, young woman. I'll see what I can do.'

"**A**ND THE NEXT DAY, *rabboisai*, he's back, all smiles. 'You're not going to believe this, young woman. A transport arrived yesterday, and there was a *mohel* on it!' But then, suddenly he gets very serious. 'Young woman,' he says, 'I don't know what kind of *zechus* you have, but Somebody wants that *yingel* of yours to have a *bris*. I met this man yesterday. He's not only a *mohel*; he's also a rav and a *shochet*.

"'Anyway, I tell him the story. He says he doesn't have his knife, his *mohel messer*. Before he left, he managed to pack only his *chalef*, his slaughtering knife. After all, he thinks, a Jew never knows where he might find himself and what he might need. So he packed his *chalef* before he left, but he didn't manage to pack his *mohel messer*. So I say to him that we have surgical instruments at the hospital, and surely he could..., and before I can finish, he says he just wants to check and make sure. So he opens up his bag, and nearly faints: there's no *chalef*, only a *mohel messer*!'

"So Leah, she doesn't answer for a minute, and then she says, 'Dr. Tuchman?'

"'Yes, young woman?'

"'Would you be *kvater*?'

❦

"**A**ND THAT'S HOW IT WAS, *rabboisai*, not so long ago, and not so far away. Our Leah'leh, she named her son Menasheh for the father of her husband, and she prayed that God should give her the strength to lead her pure little boy to *Torah, chupah*, and *maissim toivim*. And when you cried, Menasheleh, when you cried at your first *bris*, do you know what your mother said to you? 'Don't cry,' she said. 'When you turn thirteen, I'll make you a real *simcha*. Your father and I together. We'll make you a *bris* like nobody ever saw.'"

And then the stranger whispers, "And you know what, Menasheleh? You stopped crying."

"Oy, Menasheleh, my Menasheleh," he sings, choking now on his own tears. "Do you see, Menasheleh? Do you understand that this is not only your bar mitzva, but the *simcha* of those who never made it? The celebration of those whose mothers didn't have the strength yours did, and those unblessed with your good fortune. And Menasheleh, it is also the second *bris* your mother promised you. Do you understand what had to happen so that you could have your first *bris* at the proper time? Can you fathom what *mesirus nefesh* that was? Do you see what being a Jew means to your mother and meant to so many *heiligeh Yiddin* who did not come back? Do you understand your great *zechus* and your great obligations?"

Then suddenly he stops, this strange man. He looks slowly around the room. He coughs twice, removes a grimy handkerchief from his pocket, blows his nose loudly, and resumes talking. His voice becomes louder. His green eyes begin to sparkle. His right thumb begins tracing great arcs in the air, and the sing-song becomes even more pronounced.

"And the cigarettes, *rabboisai*, what ever happened to all of Leah'leh's cigarettes? What's a *bris* without a *seudah*? She traded those cigarettes for enough bread that at least ten men could eat a few morsels. I know, because I had a couple of crumbs myself. And she traded for some wine, an onion, some half-rotten potatoes, a bit of salt, a couple of eggs — very expensive items, eggs — and who knows what else. And somehow — to this day I don't know where she baked it, she said it was her secret — she made a kugel. And believe me, *rabboisai*, if you think the kugels of Williamsburg are *geshmak*, that kugel, *rabboisai*, that kugel that Leah'leh prepared for us there in that Nazi hell had *ta'am Gan Eden*."

Heard from: Mrs. Devorah Ess

A Moving Episode

HE JULY 4TH weekend was approaching and Shlomie and Chavi Weinstein and their brood of seven were preparing for their annual pilgrimage to "the Mountains." Variously known as "the country" or "the Borscht Belt," their destination would be more readily located on a map under the designation Catskill Mountains. For most of the year, the Jewish population of this resort area is virtually nil, but during the summer it fairly teems with urban Jews fleeing to its rural surroundings and cooler climate only two-and-a-half hours (without traffic) away from civilization.

It might seem odd that hordes of religious Jews so willingly — even enthusiastically — abandon spacious, comfortable homes to crowd into dilapidated, mosquito-infested bungalows without so much as a telephone, not to mention other amenities. Be that as it may, since time immemorial, a vacation in the Mountains has always been the highlight of the year for countless families.

Since the idea is to get away from the City, families understandably pack anything and everything they might conceivably need for the entire two-month R 'n R: adequate clothing, pots and pans, plates, cutlery, recreational paraphernalia, reading matter, toys — you name it. Packing for this temporary relocation seems to bear all the symptoms, trappings, and trauma of a permanent move across the ocean.

In fact, the only obvious difference between a permanent move and the summer move to the Mountains is that the former is usually executed by professional, experienced movers equipped with the appropriate gear, brawn, and vehicles, while the latter is traditionally a homespun project of amateur movers with names like Shlomie, Chavi, Malki, Ruchie, Chaim, Naomi, and so on.

The Weinstein bunch did the packing, but since they did not own a car (not that everything would have ever fit into one), Chavi did some comparison shopping for van drivers. Her Yellow Pages were distinctively annotated with scribbles and jottings next to the names of drivers she had employed in previous years. Chavi's editorial comments ranged from "rip-off" to "reckless," and everyone so designated shared the ignominious fate of never being patronized by the Weinsteins again.

THIS YEAR the firm of Gonzalez Bros. came in with the lowest bid and was hired for the job. Pedro Gonzalez, junior partner in this booming conglomerate, arrived only two-and-a-half hours late on Thursday afternoon.

"I wuss havin' some problem wit de troke," Pedro apologized meekly. But this was no consolation for the Weinsteins, who had planned to arrive in the Mountains in time to unpack that evening and be able to prepare leisurely for Shabbos the following day.

Moreover, Pedro chose an unusually scenic route that took in all the picturesque urban areas of the Big Apple, especially the ones the Weinsteins had studiously avoided until then. How Pedro managed to include Brownsville, East New York, Bedford Stuyvesant, the Bowery, Spanish Harlem, Washington Heights, and the South Bronx in his mysterious flight plan was a geographical achievement of the highest order, unduplicable by even the most inventive New York cabbie.

Throughout, the diminutive Mexican expatriate crooned in a foreign tongue to his rusting, antiquated van as a mother to her child, cajoling it to perform vehicular feats obviously well beyond its capability, such as starting up again after pausing for a red light. Reduced to awestruck silence by some of the more exotic sights along the way, the Weinsteins mentally joined their driver's engine-encouraging. But to no avail: in the section of the Bronx affectionately known as "Fort Apache," Pedro's wheezing old Chevy spluttered its final phlegmatic cough.

IF YOU HAD TO pick the last place in the world where you would want your car to break down, this would unmistakably be it. On one side of the street were low buildings framed by the jagged remnants of grimy window panes and crowned by spirals of razor wire. The last visitors these abandoned storefronts had seen were arson investigators, and their sooty brick facades formed one giant canvas for spray-can artists like the "Savage Nomads," who had staked out this part of the Bronx as their personal turf.

On the other side of the street was one of the nation's busiest pharmaceutical operations, though the crack dealers who worked there were strictly freelance and off the books. The few pedestrians on the chewed-up street were all clad in T-shirts, jeans, and multicolored high-top sneakers with limp laces and lolling tongues that bopped to the beat of their boom boxes. And they all had a cool, blank, intractable look which was anything but welcoming.

A few teenagers began to converge on the van, and Pedro realized that he had better summon the cavalry — PRONTO! He instructed Shlomie to watch the van (no reference to the humans inside) and ran to a phone booth. Since the South Bronx was not too far from the Gonzalez Bros. global headquarters, help was dispatched within one terrifying hour. In the interim, perhaps because of the Spanish inscriptions on the sides of the van, or, more likely, owing to the fervent *Tehillim* recitations in the hearts of its occupants, the Weinsteins suffered nothing more intimidating than a curious finger or two pointed in their direction.

GERALDO GONZALEZ came barreling by in the kind of twenty-foot frigate they stopped manufacturing in 1975. It came screeching and nose-diving to a halt alongside Pedro's van, made a klutzy about-face, and parked directly in front of the vehicle. Geraldo opened the hood while Pedro entertained him with an unending slew of verbiage and gesticulation. Under the chemical yellow of a sodium vapor street lamp, the two technocrats tinkered with what passed for the engine as Chavi made a mental note not to even annotate this van company in the Yellow Pages but to excise it altogether with her nail scissors.

Eventually, Pedro boarded his chariot and informed his horrified passengers that he was ready to continue now that the vehicle had been pronounced street-worthy. But, as they say, "Man toils and God foils." With a generous helping of Divine intervention, the van made it all the way across the George Washington Bridge before it gasped its final breath. Although the Port Authority officials declared it D.O.A., the vacationers were profoundly grateful that this fatal breakdown had not occurred on hostile turf.

Reluctant to perform the last rites, Gonzalez got on the horn to his Bros. while the Weinsteins ventured out to the shoulder of the road. No sooner had they escaped their metal prison than a convoy of coreligionists stopped to offer assistance. No fewer than seven cars had pulled over, all of whose available passenger and trunk space was pressed into service to get the Weinsteins and their luggage to Monsey, where they would have to make a pit stop for the night.

All the neophyte chauffeurs were headed for Monsey and all of them competed for the privilege of hosting the Weinsteins overnight. An orderly transfer was arranged and the caravan departed, leaving Pedro to await another Gonzalez to bail him out. Either he or one of his amigos would pick them up in Monsey in the morning.

JORJE GONZALEZ arrived at 11:30 AM (a mere three-and-a-half hours late) in what appeared to be a miraculous resurrection of the very same dearly departed van that Pedro had driven. Everyone loaded up and settled down for what was hoped would be the final leg of this family excursion to the Mountains.

But the Weinsteins weren't the only ones heading out of the City, and the traffic on the Quickway (a wishful misnomer for any thoroughfare on the Friday afternoon of July Fourth weekend) proceeded at a pace somewhere between "slow go" and "no go." Occasionally the congestion eased just long enough for jubilant motorists to accelerate to a dizzying five miles an hour.

Jorje's van didn't take very kindly to the stop-and-go traffic. Not that the horses under the hood were champing at the bit, anxious to be given free rein. On the contrary, those horses should have been put out to pasture long ago. No, the problem had something to do with the carburetor, fuel line, piston rings, valves, and fan belt. Outside the city of Monroe, the "troke" croaked and ground to a dead halt. But once again, aid was not long in coming: a chassidic resident of Monroe beheld the Weinsteins' plight and hurried to the rescue.

Reb Chassid the savior (who would not identify himself) did not ask what to do; he simply took charge. He instructed Chavi and the children to pile into his car and told them that he was sending a van service from Monroe to immediately retrieve their belongings. In the meantime, he was taking the family to his house in town to refresh themselves while Shlomie and Jorje stayed behind to man the fort.

EN ROUTE, Reb Chassid got busy with his cellular phone, sounding for all the world like a Yiddish-speaking state trooper. Once in Monroe, he jumped out of the car every time he spotted a van or a large station wagon parked along the way. It didn't take Chavi long to realize that there *was* no van service in Monroe; Reb Chassid had only said that so as to put the distraught family at ease. Now he was trying to cajole anyone he saw into driving the Weinsteins closer to their destination in the few hours left before Shabbos.

Reb Chassid had no children of his own yet and his house was immaculate. The parquet floor gleamed and there was not a speck of dust to be seen or a single thing out of place. Except for Chavi's children, who were sticky from spent Popsicles, speckled with rice cake crumbs, and eager to run amok after being cooped up all day in a smelly van. She tried valiantly to keep them from climbing on their hosts' exquisite matching crushed velvet sofas, but the smiling saints themselves lifted the children onto the couches.

Reb Chassid brought out an armful of soda bottles and beckoned all the little Weinsteins (or in this case, Soda Stains) over to the table, which was already set for Shabbos and covered with a beautiful, hand-embroidered linen tablecloth. Within seconds it was impossible to tell that this cloth had once been white, as seven pairs of filthy elbows and grubby hands massaged rivulets of spilled raspberry and cream soda into the defenseless fabric.

But the hosts were neither offended nor upset. On the contrary, they acted as if they actually enjoyed the whole mess. Mrs. Chassid excused herself, then reappeared with a scrumptious cake fresh from the oven, which had obviously been baked for Shabbos. While she served everyone a generous slice, her husband took his leave to resume his search for a "van service."

BY THE TIME the children had completed their assault on the cake (and the tablecloth) Reb Chassid returned to announce that everything had been arranged. He helped the Weinsteins back into his car and was off. But instead of returning to Shlomie and the van (of blessed memory), he continued up the highway toward the bungalow colony.

Chavi was speechless. Not only had an anonymous stranger rescued and fed her family, but, with just a few hours left before Shabbos, he was abandoning home and hearth to battle the weekend traffic for them.

Yet as they sped toward the mountains, she was frightfully concerned for her husband and all their worldly goods held ransom in Jorje's heap of spare parts. She had absolutely everything in that van, from diapers to Shabbos candles. But what could she say? Even to mention her husband would be to exhibit unforgivable ingratitude. Whatever the expense, even if it meant half their summer budget to hire three local taxis, poor Shlomie would have to fend for himself.

The snarl of traffic played on Chavi's nerves. As anyone ever caught in a Friday afternoon traffic jam knows, the feeling of utter helplessness is enough to make one cry. It looked like they would make it to the bungalow in time for Shabbos, but how would her gracious driver make it back to Monroe? Chavi assumed that Reb Chassid was probably drawing the same conclusion and in a minute or two would announce that he was giving up and turning back. But nothing of the sort happened. Reb Chassid pressed on, saving seconds by artfully cutting and edging forward in whichever lane offered a momentary opening.

In the end, the dauntless driver got the Weinsteins to the ramshackle entrance of the Maurice bungalow colony only fifty-two minutes before Shabbos. A cheering crowd of "country cousins," worried sick over the Weinsteins' tardiness, were on hand to greet them. And pulling up alongside Reb Chassid's car was a heavily laden station wagon driven by a Reb Chassid look-alike. Out from under the jumble of suitcases, cartons, and shopping bags emerged a squashed but smiling Shlomie.

A CADRE of able-bodied boys swiftly unloaded the wagon and formed a human chain from the vehicle to the steps of the Weinsteins' bungalow, such that each item went from door to door in sixty seconds. And not a second too soon: their anonymous driver and his escort had precious little time to race back to Monroe. Fortunately there was no southbound traffic to impede them.

With only fifty minutes until candle-lighting, there was hardly time for elaborate farewells. All Shlomie could do was express his sincere gratitude and offer to pay for all the costs incurred. But his words fell on screeching tires. "The Rebbe taught us to perform acts of *chessed* whenever we can," the driver called out the window as he spun his car around. And thus, leaving no clue to their identity, he and his comrade burned rubber back to Monroe.

Shlomie and Chavi looked at each other with disbelieving eyes. "Who was that bearded man?" was the unspoken question of the day. But there was little time for contemplation — Shabbos was just around the corner!

"**R**ELAX!" a neighbor ordered. "Look in your kitchen. We've already prepared Shabbos for you; you have nothing to worry about." Chavi's relief was total. Collapsing in a lawn chair, she allowed the day's pent-up tears of tension and frustration to flow unchecked.

"It must have been some day," another of the assembled remarked sympathetically. "How do you feel?"

Chavi reviewed in her mind all the kind Jews who had stopped and helped them since the George Washington Bridge: the strangers who had been their hosts in Monsey, the Chassidic couple from Monroe who had given whatever they possibly could and more, the driver of the station wagon who had pitched in to help them in their time of need, and all those who had been considerate enough to prepare the Shabbos meals for them.

"How do I feel?" Chavi laughed. "Like hanging a sign around my neck that reads, '*Mi k'amcha Yisrael?*'"

Heard from: Mrs. Shaindy Siegfried, Mrs. Esther Alter, Yechiel Rhein

And These Bones Shall Live

DOVID NEWMAN arrived on time at his rendezvous point; his father's train would take an extra half hour. A diligent student in northern England's Gateshead Yeshiva, he had coordinated with his father, who lived in London, that they would meet in York, a city approximately midway between the two locations. With half an hour to kill, Dovid gave in to his curiosity about the city he had passed through so many times on his way to yeshiva but never actually visited. Eagerly, he set out to investigate.

A shadow of shame hovers over the city of York, where no Jew has lived since 1189. The site of one of the bloodiest massacres in Jewish history, York was placed in *cherem* by the rabbis and Jewish habitation there was banned forever.

DOVID STEPPED OUT of the terminal and a steady breeze hugged his shoulders. He turned up his collar, anchored his hat with a firm tug, and proceeded down one of the streets that intersected the area around the station. Taking in all the shops on the block, the boy merged with the pulsating noontime crowds that swirled and surged and then clustered at corners, waiting for the lights to change.

The din of heavy earth-moving equipment on a side street caught his attention and brought out the child within him. The fascination of watching any kind of motorized apparatus or machinery had never lost its allure for Dovid Newman.

The adventurous yeshiva student quickly abandoned his tour and focused exclusively upon the site of a Sainsbury car park under construction. Boards had not yet been erected to fence off the area, and Dovid had a sidewalk view of the earth being teased, pushed, and then scooped out in great hopperfuls. The backhoe's thickly treaded tires, apparently unable to decide in which direction to head, bounced and crested over the increasingly furrowed ground. Headlights rattling, the vehicle retraced its path over the terrain, its motorized whine rising to a grumbling roar as its great, voracious claw arched and then bit deeply into the unresistant soil. The giant shovel, agape and drooling earth clumps, was maneuvered to a nearby truck and lowered to release the captured soil, which cascaded into the truck's waiting bin.

"Stop! Stop!" Dovid found himself suddenly shouting. He drew the attention of some passersby, but the driver, mesmerized by the rhythmic bleep-bleep, bleep-bleep warning that the behemoth was in reverse, was oblivious to his cries. As the operator shifted gears to roll forward, Dovid began waving his arms like animated windshield wipers and running back and forth to catch the driver's eye.

In his frenzy, Dovid rushed heedlessly forward to the edge of the work-site, his shoes sinking quickly into the crumbling soil. Arms windmilling, the boy lost his balance and rolled down into the newly dug pit, his ungraceful somersaults halting mere feet from the claws of the insatiable shovel. Like a mole scurrying up its tunnel, he madly emerged from the dirt, gulped some air, and finally captured the operator's attention. The man quickly turned off the engine and climbed down from the cab.

"What's up, mate?" he asked the boy who had nearly gotten scooped up by his shovel. "Dja lose yer marbles, then, wot?"

Dovid could barely get a straight sentence out because of his excitement. "Look! Look over there!" he gasped, pointing with his whole body and positioning himself so precariously that he almost fell over again. "You're digging up bones! Can't you see? This must've been a cemetery!"

"Blimey!" the operator breathed, mopping his brow with a grimy handkerchief and shaking his head in wonderment. "Coo, but I don't want to be doin' that. I'm not one much fer even bein' in a churchyard meself, what with all them graves and all. What'd me missus, her bein' Church of England loik, what'd she say to this I shouldn't loik ta know, it just 'avin' been All Soul's Day and 'ere's me diggin' up some poor soul's bones without even knowin' it."

A CROWD BEGAN TO FORM and tongues wagged excitedly. The centers of attention were the yeshiva student, the steamshovel operator, and the dump truck driver who had joined the symposium. Expeditions of bystanders made forays below street level to examine the evidence. With only slightly less restraint than the others, Dovid bent down and pushed aside some dirt, uncovering what appeared to be sections of a skeleton. It was very clear to this sensitive soul that the digging must desist at once; unfortunately, Dovid Newman was not overseeing this particular project.

Soon, an official-looking van pulled up and a man carrying a clipboard emerged. The shovel operator hurried over to him to present his report of the goings-on, punctuating his words with frequent finger-jabs aimed at young Dovid.

Taking charge of the pandemonium, the foreman sauntered over to the boy. Determined to put an end to the slowdown before it developed into a full-blown moratorium, he faced the troublemaker menacingly and opened his mouth to scold, but he never got a chance.

Dovid had been contemplating how he could ascertain if these bones were actually human when the obvious solution came to him in a flash. Before the foreman's intended tirade passed his lips, Dovid yelled to the operator, "Don't do any more digging until I get back!" Then, as if running for his life, he dashed off.

The lunch-hour crowd had swelled to a full-blown throng by this time, all eyes riveted to the impromptu street theater. Sensing their mood, the foreman wisely backed down and held his peace. Surely the delay would be brief, he told himself, and not worth his going against what might turn into an ugly mob.

DR. STANLEY NEWMAN walked the length of the terminal and back again in search of his son. He had already verified that Dovid's train had arrived on schedule and he knew his boy was not the type to engage in mischief in order to pass the time. Concern for Dovid's well-being began to gnaw at him.

Dovid raced at last through the entrance of the train station and sped to the center of the lobby. The boy was a mess: his face was dirt-streaked, his shoes scuffed beyond recognition, and dark brown soil nearly obliterated the pinstripe of his suit. At the sight of him, Dr. Newman was overcome with relief and that tremendous feeling of love and pride for the youngster who had reached the edge of adolescence and was soon to be a man. Whatever the explanation for his tardiness and appearance, Dr. Newman was certain that it would be the truth. His boy would not equivocate.

But Dovid offered neither explanation nor excuse for his lateness, nor did he apologize for the way he looked. In a very agitated tone and with all the eagerness of a puppy tugging at his owner's trouser leg to come and see his find, Dovid begged his father to follow him. There was no point in resisting, and curiosity was already doing its share to insure Dr. Newman's compliance. Only something of great import would cause Dovid's natural courtesy to be supplanted by such urgency. Dr. Newman grabbed his bag and followed.

BY THE TIME the Newmans had arrived the crowd had trebled in size. Two policemen were attempting to withstand the surging masses and prevent mayhem, urging the bystanders to "Step back. Step back," an incantation that had no visible effect.

"I'm a doctor," Dovid's father announced. "How can I help?" As they'd hurried breathlessly through the streets of York, Dovid had given his father a sketchy outline of the events at the construction site.

"'Fraid yer a mite late, guv," the steamshovel operator noted congenially. "These chaps 'ave no need o' yer services now, 'ave they?"

One of the bobbies approached. "You can have a look if you like, sir, seeing as how you're a doctor, but please don't touch anything. We've already radioed headquarters for assistance."

TREKKING AFTER DOVID to the deepest ditch in the ground, Newman eased himself into the hollow. His expression was serious and professional as he peered at the stick-like protrusions peeking out of the earth like a macabre species of vegetation. There was no question about his son's find: the ground was sown with human remains of ancient vintage. The bones were yellowed, even though the soil so deep down was dry.

As the assembled speculated noisily on what historical site had just been inadvertently unearthed, a far more sobering thought shot through Dr. Newman's head. From the little he knew of York, the train station was situated in what was known as the "Jewbury district," although Jews had not lived in York for centuries. The doctor shared his insight with his son and the boy's eyes grew rounder as he began to absorb the full significance of his father's remark.

"It is premature to make any assumptions," Dr. Newman said, "but I should like to contact the rabbinic authorities straight away." He exchanged words with the police officers and their superiors, who had arrived in the interim, then followed their directions to the nearest call box.

Left by himself to hold the fort, Dovid's mind began to wander. The crush of the crowd and the sounds of the traffic faded as the memory of a fifth-grade lesson about the Jews of York suddenly flooded his head. Dovid looked at the ground below and imagined he heard the voice of Yosef ben Avraham crying out to him from the depths.

"**M**UMMY, Mummy, I'm home," Yosef ben Avraham called as he turned the corner of Jewbury Street. His family's house was in the heart of York's Jewish district, and Yosef knew it would please his mother that he'd arrived. His mother, however, in the midst of her Pesach cleaning and preparations, did not respond. She could hear nothing outside of her kitchen. And even if there had not been so much distraction within the house itself, she would never have been able to make out anything above the commotion that was taking place on the steps.

Entering the narrow alley between the houses, Yosef, too, heard the ruckus. He rounded the corner and began to mount the stairs, where he discovered his younger sister, Sara, holding a bun just out of baby Yonah's reach. The two-year-old was shrieking and squalling and trying to wrest the cake from his sister's sticky hand.

"What are you doing to him?" Yosef demanded.

"I am not teasing him, if that's what you think. Yonah wants a cake and Mummy said he's not to get the crumbs all over. The only place where he may eat it is out in the street." Then, with a grand concession to the obvious, she continued, "He just doesn't want to wait till we get outside."

"Come, my little messer," Yosef said cheerfully as he swung Yonah under his arm like a sack of wheat. "Let's get you outside in a hurry. Thump, thump, thump!" He bounded down the stairs with a giggling Yonah and an eager Sara clopping right behind. Yonah's cooperation was rewarded with a fistful of cake for each hand.

AS IF Yosef were interested, Sara began to update her brother on the day's Pesach progress. "All of the bedrooms have been completed and only the kitchen remains to be cleaned. The silver has been polished and all your hose and jerkins have been shaken out and refolded. And what have *you* been doing all day?" she challenged.

Yosef knew that he shouldn't respond, but the temptation was too strong to resist. "Even girls," he began in an authoritative tenor, "should know about the riots at the time of King Richard's coronation last September. Father says that Benedict and Joce are the richest and most important Jews in all of York, yet they were denied entry into the abbey and the palace to deliver gifts from the Jewish communities to the king. The mob beat them and dragged them away and poor Benedict was taken into a church and baptized against his will. When King Richard learned of this, he was distressed, but that didn't help out Benedict, since he died from his wounds."

Sara nodded pensively. It was her first bitter taste of what it meant to be a Jew in York. She had always imagined that King Richard loved his Jews.

YOSEF wished to awaken her to reality. "Maybe we need some Jewish knights to fight back," he said, his small fists clenched.

"Well, we can't have any because knights have to go to church and do all of that. And anyways," the little girl added pragmatically, "you're too young to be a knight."

Yosef continued as if he had not been interrupted. "Even if father has never revealed anything to us, I know that he has been out at meetings. I wish I knew what they were planning."

"Do *you* have a plan?" Sara's eyes narrowed, and were at once both knowing and teasing. Her emphasis on the "you" was in the mocking little-sister lilt that has been the scourge of older brothers for generations.

Accepting the challenge, Yosef assumed the offensive. "Have you been snooping through my things? Do I have to turn you upside down to make you tell?" As Yosef's tone grew more insistent, Yonah began to wail, indicating that his bun had been reduced to a mass of soggy crumbs.

Red spots burned in the seven-year-old's cheeks. "You shan't make me talk, even if you torture me like the Crusaders! So there, Master High and Mighty. You are just plain Yosef of Jewbury Street and—" she paused, taking a breath before playing out her parting shot, "and you only have a stinky old catapult, la, la, la, la, la, la."

Impelled by indignation and emboldened by his fascination with Jewish history, Yosef countered, "King David also only had a catapult, yet he was able to defeat the giant. He was the hero of Israel!"

Despite his bravado, Yosef was as frightened as his sister was. Yonah's wail slid into a higher octave, and as much to break the tension as to hush the toddler, Yosef scooped him up and walked him about.

"**Y**OSEF." Asher ben Avraham's voice was weary, and that disturbed his son far more than the normally stern cadence his father reserved for dealing with those miscreants who were playing when they should have been learning or working. "Come here."

Yosef handed Yonah to Sara and went to his father's side.

"Sit down next to me," Asher began. "It is time that I talk with you. You are the eldest of the children, and will soon be bar mitzva."

Yosef blushed in acknowledgment of his father's words.

"I realize you know what is happening. Since the time of William of Normandy and for over one hundred years God has blessed us with peace and prosperity here in England. But now there are those who would eagerly take away both blessings. You have heard, no doubt, of the riots last fall."

Yosef nodded solemnly.

"Those riots were not the end of our troubles, but the beginning. Even though King Richard tried to control the mobs and even issued an edict protecting the Jews, the moment he left on his crusade, his subjects grew uncontrollable.

"Only a month ago, after the Jews of Lynn were attacked, our brothers in Norwich were victimized. We have just heard that the Jews of Stamford, two days to the south, have also been pillaged. Only those who could escape to the castle were saved, but their homes and all of their possessions were looted."

ASHER SIGHED HEAVILY and then paused in his dire monologue to look at his son. "The worst is yet to come. Not only is the danger spreading north, but with each episode the riots intensify. Word has arrived from Lincoln, which is only one day's ride from here, that the community is under siege. Most of the Jews were able to flee to the castle and they have sent us an urgent warning to do the same!"

Yosef's heart beat faster. The gravity of his father's tone underscored the frightening specter of his words. "We have been meeting at the rabbi's house to work on a plan. We may have to leave our homes at any moment. I need to be able to count on you to help in any way I ask. Without argument, without explanation."

The boy dropped his gaze, knowing how many times he had balked at certain tasks, sulked, or simply disappeared and not done what he'd been asked.

"I need you to do whatever your mother requires without causing any difficulties. You are not to tease your sisters and brothers or create any disturbances. At this moment we need harmony in our house and among our people." Asher recited his last request in a gentle, wistful voice, almost like a prayer. Yosef nodded his commitment and the full measure of love and trust apparent in his father's eyes was now mirrored in his own.

"I will help even without being asked," Yosef pledged. Asher swept his son into an emotional, wordless embrace and then went upstairs to apprise his wife of the recent events.

L IKE AN EVIL APPARITION, word of the imminent danger spread throughout the Jewish quarter that night and the following day. Shabbos came, but even the tranquility which always accompanied the Sabbath Queen could not dispel the tension that enveloped the close-knit community. Before the conclusion of the prayer-filled Shabbos, Rabbi Yom Tov bar Isaac of Joigny — the rabbi of York, who had immigrated from France — exhorted his flock to have greater faith in the Almighty and accept His will.

All too quickly the uneasy calm that had permeated the day of rest gave way to the flicker of the *Havdalah* candles, which revealed ominous shadows stalking the streets. The moment the Sabbath ended, each of the families wended their way under the starless sky. Silently, so as not to draw attention to themselves, and laden with their children and whatever valuables they could carry out of the Jewbury district, they slipped into the sanctuary of Clifford's Tower, the most prominent section of the castle.

And not a moment too soon. Suddenly, the entrance to the Jewbury district began to glow with the fires of hundreds of torches as blazes devoured the largest and stateliest house. Shouts of "Fire! Fire!" and "Benedict's house is burning! Benedict's house is burning!" filled the air. Smoke and flames poured forth from the windows as timber and thatch were engulfed in the inferno.

BENEDICT'S WIDOW, too frightened to answer the pounding on the door, had been swept aside with a stunning blow when the door was finally broken down. Her oldest daughter stood aghast, hiding behind the curtain. Just six months ago she had lost her father at the hands of a hate-crazed, bloodthirsty mob, and now, before her eyes, was a grizzly reenactment.

Forcing their way into the house and destroying everything along the way, the ruffians accosted the widow and demanded, "Where is the gold, old woman?" But Mrs. Benedict was incapable of responding. The daughter, wishing to save her shell-shocked mother, pointed to the bottom of the bureau. Some of the horde ransacked the gold while others scavenged the rest of the closet. Silver candlesticks, a candelabra, and *kiddush* cups were stuffed under shirts or into sacks. Gold-embroidered Sabbath tablecloths, silk *challah* covers, and lace Sabbath shawls were strewn about the room and trampled underfoot. The casket of gold coins and the cache of gold bars were revealed, but instead of satisfying the beasts it only seemed to escalate the frenzy. When the brave girl tried to protect her mother from the merciless blows being showered on her, she, too, was attacked — with a dagger.

The rapacious mob trampled on, not even bothering to step over the lifeless bodies, in search of other "infidels" within the home. They soon found their victims, girls age seven and four huddled together in a bed. Every room was sacked, every article of furniture overturned and smashed, and for the final touch, a torch was set to the wispy netting that hung around the bed where two little girls cowered in terror.

The fire leapt to the curtains and consumed its way across the room. The marauders seemed to delight in the screams of the children burning alive. Some lingered to relish the torture but the others beat a hasty retreat. Fanned by the draft created by the open door the fire spread rapidly. When the last pillagers emerged triumphant from what was left of the house they were cheered by a jubilant crowd that had gathered in the blood-drenched street.

With the fire's hellish light reflecting on his ashen face, Asher ben Avraham hastily led his family down the alley away from their house. Carrying whatever clothes and food they could, his wife and three daughters struggled with their burdens. The baby was asleep in Yosef's arms while the four-year-old, terrified at the sight of the ubiquitous flames, buried his head in his father's shoulder. All were heavily laden with sacks which impeded their progress.

The raging fire and the menacing crowd that chanted, "The fires of Hell for the unbelieving Jews!" propelled the hundreds of families toward the castle, wreaking havoc with what was to have been a carefully orchestrated exodus.

WITH THE FIRST RAYS OF DAWN, those Jews fortunate enough to have escaped saw that the fire's fury was now spent. Nonetheless, the charred remains were still smoldering and the pocked, blackened foundations of houses on Jewbury Street looked like rows of rotted teeth. A few houses remained standing but their doors and windows had been ripped off their hinges or smashed by the frenzied looters.

The searing, choking smell of charred wood and ashes hung heavy in the morning air and was swept with each breeze into Clifford's Tower, serving as an acrid reminder of what had transpired the night before and what loomed ahead.

Early that day, Rabbi Yom Tov summoned Joce, the community's wealthiest member and most esteemed lay leader, and Asher ben Avraham to assess the situation. Because of their foresight and planning, five hundred souls had been spared, but provisions were frightfully low. The venerable rabbi directed that all the food and drink be pooled so that it could be cautiously rationed. All weapons were also to be held in common, and everyone was to take turns guarding the parapets. Needless to say, everyone's fervent prayers would continue unabated.

NO SOONER had the rabbi finished issuing his instructions than the watchman sounded the alarm. Charging across the fields was a malevolent mob wielding pitchforks, knives, swords, and lances. Apparently, the carnage of the night before had not sated their lust for blood and booty.

At their head strode a monk in white robes, lending religious passion to their "cause." Before the castle walls he addressed his fanatic followers, inciting them to greater fury: "The Jews are damned! They think that they can hide and thereby escape the hand of judgment. But we are the agents of Heaven! We shall teach them that no infidel should dare to spit on the cross of our savior! Heaven will not bless our glorious crusade to the Holy Land until we have rid England of these heretics!"

The monk then turned toward his victims and issued this appeal: "Cursed Jews — come out at once and accept the Church by baptism or go to your deaths in Hell. Your gold and your great houses, built with money you stole from fine, upstanding Christians with your usurious interest, will not help you now. Nothing will save you. Come out and answer for all your sins or we will storm the walls!"

The response of the Jews was not long in coming. A hail of rocks and stones rained down from the parapets, striking some of the barbarians below. But the mob did not retreat; instead, they began to fell trees for battering rams to attack the castle gate.

T HE TERROR of that Sunday seemed like it would never end, and confinement within the castle's massive walls brought more fear than security. Monday morning the white-robed monk returned with his crusaders and resumed his unholy quest. "My brethren, we must remain steadfast! Our mission is a sacred one! We must persevere until the evil Jews have suffered their deserved punishments! The scoundrels must not be allowed to rob good Christians anymore! Unless they accept the Church, they shall die!"

Inside the tower, Yosef sought out his father. "Why do they say such things about us, Father? We do not steal from them."

The boy's naivete broke Asher's heart. "My son," he said, "this is one of the cruel ironies of our People. Through the governments' taxes and laws, they have made it well nigh impossible for anyone who does not accept their religion to earn a living. Our taxes are higher than theirs, and we are banned from every guild and forbidden to own land.

"These restrictions leave us only one avenue of existence: the odious profession of money-lending. Whenever we provide a loan, it must be recorded in the cathedral of York so that these sums can also be levied, in addition to the other exorbitant tariffs imposed upon us. And even after we've paid the taxes, there is always the risk that the loan will never be repaid.

"It is painfully obvious that the monstrous hordes outside are not motivated merely by religious zeal. They wish to murder us and destroy any evidence of their loans. If they succeed, God forbid, their next stop will be the cathedral, to burn all the records."

Asher's dismal explanation was interrupted by the watchman's cry that the warden of the castle had somehow left the tower and was seen mingling with the attackers. When he tried to regain admission into the fortress, it was denied him for the risk was too great and his allegiance too uncertain.

THE GRUELING SIEGE continued and the brave defenders withstood the onslaught as best they could. But more insidious enemies lurked within: hunger and thirst began to stalk the Jews. By Thursday it still hadn't rained and the barrels were empty, leaving the captives bereft of both a vital fluid and a valuable weapon.

When the sheriff of York arrived with a large contingent of soldiers to support the warden in his demand to repossess the tower, there was neither water nor oil to be boiled and poured over the parapets to repel those scaling the walls. The only arsenal remaining was the stones from the inner ramparts, which could be dislodged and hurled below.

Meanwhile, the weeklong stalemate had not reduced the attackers' ardor. Every day their spiritual leader continued his vitriolic verbal assault on the Jews: "How can we imagine conquering the heathens of Jerusalem when these infidels ridicule us at home? If we cannot overtake this modest castle, how can we capture our holy city? Forward! We must not stop until the Jews are crushed!"

The battering ram pounded at the door with increased vigor, and attempts to scale the walls were renewed with mounting intensity. From behind the parapet Yosef watched the monk manipulate the crowd. In the din of the zealots below, the boy heard his calling and reached for a rock, placing it inside the tattered patch of his makeshift catapult. His palm was moist with fear and his heart thumped wildly.

Yosef waited for the right moment to launch his shot. Suddenly the monk turned around to see what progress was being made, and Yosef ben Avraham arose, took aim, and fired. The stone struck just below the temple and the monk fell forward, clutching his head. His hands turned crimson with blood and in minutes his body lay still and silent.

An inhuman roar coursed through the mob. Yosef leaned back against the wall, unprepared for the dizzy feeling that had overcome him.

Moments later Asher approached his son and, without reference to what had transpired, told him to join the others below. "The rabbi has called a meeting," he said, and led the still-quivering youth down the steps.

THE RABBI, his skin a pasty white from the fast he'd begun long before the others', spoke with surprising strength and unshaken faith.

"My people, we are at the end of our resources. The ways of God are mysterious, but apparently He has decided that we are to perform the most sacred mitzva of all. We must consider it a privilege to enter another chapter in the martyrdom of our People. It is far better to die as a Jew than be forced to live the life of those who so despise us. We must prefer a glorious death to an ignominious life. The pure soul our Creator has given us shall be returned to Him with our own hands."

A gasp arose from the assembled.

"Everyone shall now take leave of his family. Time is very short. Soon our holy Sabbath, *Shabbos Hagadol*, 'the great and terrifying day of the Lord,' will be upon us. We must finish our—" and here he paused, "preparations before the Sabbath begins."

A slaughtering knife was passed to Joce, who left the room to begin the sacred task, his face a grim mask of determination.

Yosef gripped his father's hand tightly as they walked to where the rest of his family was huddled. His younger siblings were curled up on the ground, whimpering from hunger even in their sleep. Asher gazed at his beloved wife, who nodded in acceptance. She tried to fight back her tears but they poured down her cheeks in searing rivers. Asher warmly embraced each of his children, starting with the baby, and gently replaced them on the ground. Then he turned to his daughter and whispered tenderly, "Sara, Sara'le, it is time to say 'Shema.'" The little girl obediently recited the words for the last tear-filled time, as did the next child and the next, until he turned to his oldest son.

"I am ready, Father," Yosef proclaimed stoically and began the words that Rabbi Akiva and Rabbi Chanina ben Tradyon and Chana and her seven sons and so many countless others before him had uttered in their final moments. His voice, starting hesitantly, grew steadily more resounding until the final words rang out, *Hashem Elokeinu, Hashem Echad...*

DOVID NEWMAN and his father were on hand for the reburial of the York martyrs. Reinterred were the remains of every single Jew who had sought refuge in Clifford's Tower on that heinous day eight centuries earlier, for even those who in the end chose conversion over suicide were brutally massacred by the mob that Shabbos morning. Indeed, when the attackers managed to penetrate the castle and discovered the bodies of their intended victims, they swiftly hacked to pieces the survivors — who had willingly opened the gates for them — in order to satisfy their blood-lust. The murderers then strode to the cathedral, where they cast all of the records of their loans into the Church's sacred fires.

The day of the funeral the heat was oppressive, the hottest ever recorded in July. Despite the unbearable weather, a large crowd assembled for the services. The eulogizers noted that only among the Jewish People could a modern community pay its respects to its medieval counterpart. Dovid Newman realized that for all eternity there would be a bond linking one Jewish community to another. Intuitively he also knew that the score would somehow be settled. Even as the cathedral erected with the taxes extracted from the Jews towered over the city of York, an eerie premonition told him that this chapter of Jewish History was not yet closed.

The feeling haunted him all evening, robbing him of sleep.

That night, nearly a millennium after the Jews of York sanctified the name of God with their lives, a meteorological wonder occurred. Suddenly, out of a gray and misty moonless night a mighty bolt of lightning bore down and eradicated the stiletto spires of York's minster. The cathedral and all the evil it represented, all the evil that had been perpetrated in the name of the religion for which it stood, had at last received retribution.

Heard from: Mrs. Chaja Gittleson

Southern Comfort

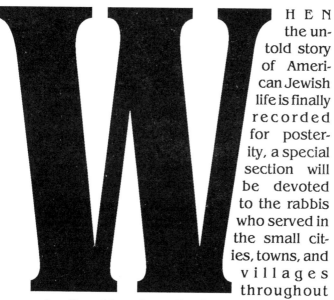

HEN the untold story of American Jewish life is finally recorded for posterity, a special section will be devoted to the rabbis who served in the small cities, towns, and villages throughout the country. Beachheads on the front line of the war against assimilation, these rabbis are the unsung heroes of Judaism. They make out of town seem like it's in town.

For the uninitiated, this is an allusion to the residents of Brooklyn, New York — the "in towners" — and everyone else, who is branded an "out of towner." Actually the same distinction applies, in a less caricaturistic way, to other metropolises. Whether you live in Boston, Mass., or Bakersfield, Cal., chances are you will define your life and lifestyle by one of those two norms. Thus, "in town" is Atlanta, Cleveland, Chicago, Detroit, Pittsburgh, Los Angeles, and, above all, New York. "In town" is where you can find all the services an observant Jew needs to remain well-rounded and well-nourished.

Every "in town" has gourmet, glatt-kosher butcher shops, *shomer Shabbos* bakeries specializing in seven-layer spectacles, a veritable cornucopia of day schools and synagogues, and bookstores stocked with Judaica of every description. Needless to say, there are *mikvaos* for men and *shiurim* for women, hat stores and wig shops, kosher restaurants and fast food franchises. The urban Yellow Pages let your fingers do the walking through the *Shulchan Aruch*.

"Out of town" has a character of its own. In exotic locations like Moose-up, Montana, Killingly, Vermont, Painesville, Ohio, and Acme, Washington, the struggle to live as a Jew takes on a different dimension. Need kosher meat? You have two choices: either slaughter your own, or travel fifty, sixty, or seventy miles to get it. Want a fresh loaf of kosher bread? No problem: every kitchen is equipped with an oven and flour. Of course, if you want to *buy* fresh bread, that's a different story. To live as a Jew in a place like this is a challenge; to be a rabbi in a place like this is frustration itself.

RABBI MITCH HELLER was looking for a challenge. Young, motivated, idealistic, and above all naive, had he ever been offered a normal suburban position, he would have rejected it. He was out to change the world and unite it under the kingship of the Lord. Lofty and sublime ideas like this could get distorted in Gotham and its environs. The head of rabbinic placement in every major yeshiva thrived on the rare corps of Mitch Hellers.

Rabbi Yisrael Greenblatt couldn't seem to get enough of them. As a yeshiva administrator in charge of matching up rabbis and communities, his job defied all norms of supply and demand. Like all matchmakers he had a few divorces to his discredit, and he wished he had the manpower to avoid the same mistakes in the future.

By and large there was a pattern to the placements: the smart students went to the big city congregations, where smart *baalei battim* critically appraised their spiritual leaders. Rabbinical students from wealthy families went to wealthy congregations, who could count on their rabbis to observe the unwritten etiquette and social graces of the upwardly mobile. And what of those rabbinical candidates who were experts in neither *pilpul* nor Pierre Cardin? Well, the yeshiva's head of placement services tried his best.

One day Rabbi Greenblatt received a letter that titillated his matchmaking sensibilities.

Dear Rabbi,

  The Orthodox Jewish Federation of Southwest Texas would like to inform you of an exciting employment opportunity. Please contact us at your earliest convenience to discuss the eligibility of one of your finest students for this stimulating and pivotal position.

Sincerely,

Lincoln Wolf, Ph.D.

"SOUNDS INTERESTING," Rabbi Greenblatt commented to his secretary as he reached for his file of job-seekers. "See if you can get Dr. Wolf on the phone, and we'll find out more."

The forte of his efficient office manager was phone connections. "Rabbi Greenblatt, Dr. Wolf is on the line."

"*Shalom aleichem*, Dr. Wolf. I received your inquiry today and the opening sounded so intriguing that I was curious to hear the details. We have some top-notch rabbinical students whom I am currently placing. What can you tell me about your organization? I don't think I've ever heard of it."

"Currently," an elderly voice answered in a warm but formal drawl, "the Orthodox Jewish Federation has three membahs — chahtah membahs, Ah might add: mahself, mah wife, 'n mah daughtah. We'ah hopin' to double our membahship, maybe even treble it, as soon as we can locate some moah Jews to sahn up."

"You mean there aren't any Jews where you are?" Rabbi Greenblatt gasped incredulously.

"How can you say 'any' when I just told y'all thayut there are three 'n we'ah incorporated? In fact, Ah'm sure there are plenty moah. Certainly you remembah from hah schyool biology the concept of protective coloration. Certain animals, lahk the deah 'n the tree toad, take on the culuhs of theyah envahronment as a way to survahv the dangahs of predatahs. Well, Ah reckon thayut the same thing has happened in the Sayuthwest. Between intah-marriage, assimilation, 'n suntans, it's hahd to tell who is Jewish and who ain't."

"But if no one appears to be Jewish, why do you need a rabbi?"

"Precisely because they don't *appeah* to be Jewish! If the people heah hayud a strong Jewish identity, we obviously wouldn't need one. But they don't, so we do!"

Rabbi Greenblatt tugged at his beard as he tried to fathom the doctor's reasoning, but it sailed right over his balding pate. "Excuse me, Dr. Wolf, but I still don't understand."

"Rabbi, we live in a small universituh town. Fuh twenty yeahs, Ah've been actin' ayuz the spiritual leadah for any Jewish student 'n facultuh membah who happens to wandah through. Now we'ah leavin' and we'ah lookin' for someone to take our place. We'ah willin' to pay."

"Well, what does your town have to offer? Is there a *mikva* within an hour's drive?"

"No."

"What about a synagogue?"

"Not yet."

"A store that sells kosher food?"

"Not exactluh," Dr. Wolf said sheepishly, sensing Rabbi Greenblatt's long-distance skepticism. "Rabbi, if you'ah goin' to be negative, we'll trah someplace else."

"Dr. Wolf, I am not being negative, but I *am* being realistic. Who in the world would want to go deep into some southwestern Siberia for a Jewish community that may or may not exist?"

HAD DR. WOLF replied, "Opportunities always knock," he would have been on the mark, for at just that moment Mitchell Alan Heller, save-the-world entrepreneur, rapped incessantly at the rabbinic placement office door.

Allowing neither Rabbi Greenblatt nor his secretary a chance to reply he opened the door, nodded his head, and interrupted, "Can I see you this afternoon? I've been trying to find a position, but after fourteen interviews, I've had no luck."

Yisrael Greenblatt looked down at the telephone and then stared back at the hopeful as if he were an apparition. "I think your luck is about to change."

"For better or for worse?" Mitch asked.

"I'm not sure," Rabbi Greenblatt replied under his breath. Smiling benignly, he offered, "Speak to me later today. I may just have something for you."

AFTER MITCH HELLER EXITED, the rabbinic placement officer put on his most official voice and intoned, "Dr. Wolf, I believe I indeed have a candidate. He's youthful, vibrant, and idealistic. I will let you know in a day or two, but in the meantime please prepare a list of whatever Jewish resources are locally available so that the rabbi will have a place to begin."

Later that afternoon, Rabbi Greenblatt cordially invited Mitch into his office, threw a solicitous arm around the unsuspecting rabbinical student, and related in a grandfatherly manner, "Young man, you walked in this morning at a very auspicious time."

"I did?" Mitch gushed.

"Oh, you most certainly did! It says a lot about a person if he knows just when to intrude."

Mitch blushed as the rabbi continued. "At the time, I was talking to a man who lives in a university town in Texas. In fact, this was not just any man, but," Greenblatt paused for effect, "the head of the Orthodox Jewish Federation of Southwest Texas."

"The Orthodox Jewish Federation of Southwest Texas!" Mitch repeated slowly, all atwitter over the augustness of the name.

"That's right," Greenblatt confirmed, "the one and only. Now this gentleman, Dr. Lincoln Wolf, is not only the chairman of the Federation but, as he humbly mentioned to me this morning, one of the charter members. That means he is a very influential individual down there. I don't believe I am assuming too much when I say that as far as Orthodox matters are concerned in Southwest Texas, his word goes.

"This brings us back to your luck, which I assured you was going to change. They're looking for a rabbi."

"That's great!" Mitch exclaimed, his face alight with excitement. Suddenly a sober expression overcame him. "You don't think they'll be as fussy as these other places about experience, do you?"

"Are you kid—, er, I don't think so," Rabbi Greenblatt replied, struggling to sound neutral. "I'll recommend you as just the right man for the job."

Mitch blushed again and begged, "Tell me more!"

"Before I do, let me tell you a story: A young man once interviewed for a rabbinical position in a small town. When it came to describing their community, the *baalei battim* were positively glowing about their local history and prestige. 'Did you know that all the greatest *gedolim* are buried here?!' they asked effusively. 'Rashi is buried here! The Bais Yosef is buried here! Ibn Ezra is buried here! In this place, you can find a lot of honor!'

"The young rabbi eagerly accepted the prestigious position, but it turned out to be a lot more difficult than he had anticipated. He had problems forming a *minyan* and organizing social events. He had problems with his members. He even had problems with those who weren't his members.

"One day, in a fit of frustration, he sought the blessing and intercession of all the outstanding spiritual heroes said to be laid to rest in the local cemetery. After an exhaustive search, however, he could find neither the Bais Yosef nor Rashi nor Ibn Ezra. The tyro's irritation knew no bounds. He stormed over to the man who had hired him and demanded, 'You told me that the great *gedolim* are buried here! I just investigated and they aren't!'

"'Rabbi,' the lay leader responded without the slightest twinge of guilt, 'you won't find them in the cemetery, because they're not there. They're resting on the bookshelves in the back of our synagogue. They're resting in the memories of our members and the dreams of our children. They're resting in unused *tallis* bags and in *shaimos*. Believe me, the *gedolim* are buried very deep here. And it's your job to exhume them and bring them back to life!'"

MITCH LAUGHED NERVOUSLY. "That's quite a story. I'll have to remember to use it in one of my sermons. But what does it have to do with me?"

"Everything," said Rabbi Greenblatt dramatically. "Because I'm sending you to just such a graveyard — I mean — town!"

"What?"

"Rabbi Heller, even though the world may judge things by quantity, the Jews are judged by quality. Just one *mitzva* performed by one man can mean a great deal more than you and I think. Are you man enough to assume the awesome responsibility of reaching out to the spiritually starving Jews of Southwest Texas?"

"Uh, I guess so," he fumbled, like someone about to step into a wet shoe.

"Good! I'll make all the arrangements. You can pack your bags *and* your boots. Congratulations!"

THUS, newly ordained Rabbi Mitch Heller assumed the mantle of leadership of Southwest Texas' Orthodox constituency. Upon his arrival in San Marcos, the Orthodox Jewish Federation of Southwest Texas was called into special session to greet and brief its new spiritual leader. Due to scheduling conflicts, however, only one-third of the membership was able to attend.

Dr. Wolf outlined the history, politics, and personalities of the local Jewish community. Less eloquently than his collaborator in New York, he highlighted that whatever there was in San Marcos Jewishly speaking was the best-kept secret in town. Fortunately, Rabbi Heller was the kind who took everything in stride, a disposition enhanced by the fact that this was the only job offer he had.

With something of a bombastic air, Dr. Wolf pontificated about the local potential for a good seven hours, insisting that Mitch take detailed notes of his excursus. One-and-a-half notebooks later, the chairman of the Federation asked Rabbi Heller if everything was clear.

Mitch nodded, but felt duty-bound to point out his own weaknesses: "I'm not a *chazzan*," he began. "In fact, I'm tone-deaf. I've also never conducted a funeral, and I don't consider myself qualified to *pasken* on halachic queries, but I do have," he hastened to add, "the phone numbers of some outstanding halachic authorities."

Dr. Wolf was impressed with the candidate's candor and was quick to reassure him that his shortcomings weren't really major drawbacks in that region.

" **A** CHAZZAN is only necessaruh when y'all hayuv a *minyan*, which y'all don't. As far as yo' lack of funeral experience is concerned, San Marcos really isn't a dyin' communituh. And you don't hayuv to worruh about halachic queruhs, for no one ovah heah hayuz any. People do whatevah they want."

Somehow, Wolf's reply did not put Mitch at ease. To change the subject ever so slightly, he inquired about the Jewish resource list that Rabbi Greenblatt had promised would be put together for him. "Were you able to prepare the list?"

"Rabbi, Ah did even bettah than that: I brought the resources with muh! Heah in one room, undah one roof, yup, heah they are, you have all the Jewish resources currently available. The slenduh woman walkin' in just now with the shoppin' bag is mah wahf, Linduh, and next to her is mah daughtah, Sandy. For the next three weeks we'll be happuh to help y'all in any way we can, befoah we move out of this heah wondahful area."

Well, there was no denying that San Marcos would be a challenge, but it wasn't exactly the struggle Mitch had had in mind.

R EGARDLESS, the would-be wunderkind threw himself into his work by drawing up a battle plan: First, he went to the local newspaper and radio and television stations to make sure they would announce his arrival. Second, he compiled a list of programs and services he would offer. Then he scoured the local directory for the names and addresses of every could-be, would-be, and should-be Jewish person in town. Last, he charted out a private timetable. If, after six months, he had nothing to show for his efforts, he would know that he had come to the wrong place.

Every sunny, dusty, boring week that rolled by seemed to indicate that the sole survivor of the Orthodox Jewish Federation of Southwest Texas should move north and east. Mitch made hundreds of phone calls, but the majority went like this:

"Hello, Mr. Golden, this is Rabbi—"

"Excuse me, Rabbi, but I'll bet you think I'm Jewish."

"Uh, yes."

"Well, I'm Irish."

"Very interesting. Did you know that the mayor of Dublin was once Jewish?"

"How nice. But I'm not. I am a priest. God bless you."

"Mr. Sidney Kramer, please."

"This is Sid. Who's this?"

"Rabbi Mitch Heller..."

"Robbie? Is that your first name? Never heard..."

"No. 'Rabbi' is my title. I'm a cleric."

"Make up your mind, will ya? Are you a rabbi or a clerk? Don't matter much anyway, seein' as how the office is closed now, but we're having a special on truck and van rentals next week. What were you looking for?"

"You."

"U? We don't carry U-Hauls. Sorry." Click.

"Hello, is this..."

"Marcus Mortuary, your rest is our peace."

"May I speak to Mr. Marcus, please?"

"Is this concerning a dearly departed?"

"No, I just wanted to speak to you about your heritage."

"Oh, yes, the Heritage Line, a very wise choice in caskets. Would you care for the mahogany with solid brass handles, or the oak with silver-plated handles?"

"I'm not calling about caskets."

"I see. Well we have the best selection of simulated antique urns north of the Rio Grande—"

"Mr. Marcus, please! My call has nothing to do with death. On the contrary, it's about life."

"Young man, it is very important that you come to terms with your own mortality and learn to accept death. Denial is a normal but unproductive reaction to the demise of a loved one. If you are a religious man, then I would urge you to have faith that one day you will be reunited with your dear departed, but for now you must accept."

"Thanks for the advice. I am a religious man. In fact, I'm calling about religion. I would like to study Judaism with you."

"Judaism?"

"You *are* Jewish, aren't you?"

"I am not, and I never was."

"Oh, I'm sorry. I thought that with a name like Marcus, you must be Jewish."

"Actually, Marcus is my first name. My last name is Cannibal, but Cannibal Mortuary just didn't have the right ring to it."

W HEN IT BECAME CLEAR that the success of his telephone soliciting could not justify the phone bill, Mitch tried a more flamboyant approach. He plastered the city with huge, Day-Glo-colored posters emblazoned with the following advertisement:

FELAFEL NIGHT AT SOUTHWEST TEXAS U!
MONDAY, AUGUST 8, AT 8:00 PM
ALL YOU CAN EAT FOR ONLY FOUR SHEKELS
(THAT'S JUST TWO BUCKS!)

Mitch's New York connections supplied the goods: fourteen dozen felafel balls and fifty pita breads. He advertised in the college newspaper and placed the posters in the dormitory, the library, and even the laundromat. Mitch personally prepared the middle-eastern delicacy and stacked them up row after row in expectation of the capacity crowd. "This is the big night," he kept telling himself, hoping that he would be able to give everyone at least a little personal attention.

MITCH DID A LOT of looking at his watch that night as he waited and waited for the room to fill up, or at least for one lost soul to make a cameo appearance. The level of excitement generated by Felafel Night was somewhere between watching grass grow and a coma. "Maybe I should have advertised kosher tortillas," Mitch pondered.

At ten past ten, somebody finally walked into the room. "Hey, man, is this where you got that Mexican food?"

Rabbi Heller leaped out of his chair in excitement. "Mexican food you're looking for?"

The boy nodded his head.

"Uh...*sí, sí, frijoles, chiquita, grando* and all that. This is pretty close. Come right in. My name's Mitch. What's yours?"

"Bernie. Bernie Feldman."

"Bernie, my friend," the rabbi declared, practically hugging the boy, "you're an angel from Heaven!"

"No, I'm not. I'm a dishwasher at the Torres–Balalaika restaurant. 'Angels' is the competition. My boss sent me to see if you have any Slovakian or Mexican recipes we could swipe, er, I mean, swap."

"Help yourself. Have a felafel on the house. You can have fifty if you want. Gosh, I hope you're hungry!" Bernie and the rabbi talked for a while, or to be accurate, the dishwasher nodded his head a few times to Heller's incessant questions as he munched away at the most un-Mexican dish he had ever tasted. After he'd had his fill, he excused himself, explaining that he had to get back for the late-night shift.

As Bernie tore himself away from the glamor and excitement of Felafel Night, Rabbi Heller called out, "Listen, can we get together some time?"

The puzzled dishwasher answered, "Sure, why not?" Then, as if propelled by the hot Texas air, he shot out.

"**A**T LAST," Mitch marvelled, "here is my 'Raison d'Esther,' as they say in French: a real, live Jewish kid who's interested — downright dying — to learn about his heritage!" By the time Rabbi Heller went to sleep, Bernie Feldman had grown in his mind from a casual acquaintance to a good friend, a great pal, and a close and loving *talmid*. There was just one little hitch for Mitch when he woke up in the morning: he didn't know where to find his bosom buddy.

"Oh, no!" Mitch yelped in terror. "Why didn't I ask him for his number or his address or something?" Trying to get hold of himself, he strained his brain to recall any detail that might provide a lead. At last he remembered that Bernie worked for a restaurant, but he couldn't recall which one.

No matter, Sherlock Heller would initiate an investigation that would do the Orthodox Jewish Federation of Southwest Texas proud. He would get his man yet. Yellow Pages in hand, he set off in telephonic, gastronomic hot pursuit:

"Hello, Casa de Mama? Do you have an employee named Bernie Feldman? No *comprende* English? Okay." Click.

"Hello, Almonte's Sicilian City? Would you know a busboy named Bernie Feldman?" Click.

"Hello, Eatcetera? Do you know a cook named Bernie Feldman?"

(Munch, munch, chew chew.) "Hey man, I'm eatin', bug off!"

"Hello, Mon Kee See? Do you have a maitre d' named Bernie Feldman?"

"Solly Cholly."

"Hello, Chez Pedro? Do you have a waiter named Bernie Feldman?"

"*Excusez moi, amigo.*"

A FTER CALLING NINETEEN RESTAURANTS, he reached Torres–Balalaikas. "Uh, hello. I'm looking for an individual named Bernie Feldman. He's there? *Baruch Hashem*! Uh, I mean, great!"

When the dishwasher finally splashed onto the phone, Mitch was euphoric. "Hey, Bernie!"

"Who is this?"

"Rabbi Mitch Heller! How're ya doin'?"

"Who?"

"Your buddy, Rabbi Heller. Don't you remember? We had such a nice, long talk at Felafel Night."

"Oh, yeah, you mean last night. My stomach is still killing me. What can I do for you, Rabbi?"

"The question is, what can I do for you? Do you want to get together for some learning? I can teach you Hebrew or *halacha* or *gemara.*" A rush of thoughts poured into Rabbi Heller's head and out of his mouth. Suddenly he was seized by a seasonal inspiration: "Bernie, do you know about the Nine Days?"

"Yeah, I saw them in concert once, but I'm not really into heavy metal."

"No, no. The Nine Days lead up to Tisha B'Av, the date that commemorates the destruction of the Holy Temple. Jewish people mourn during this period. We don't take showers..."

"Don't take showers? Rabbi, this is Texas, sweat city! If you don't take a shower every day, you'll die!"

"I didn't mean that kind of shower, I meant for pleasure — forget it. We'll learn something else instead."

"Hold on, Rabbi. I dropped out of school four years ago because I didn't like studying. So now if you wanna talk about music, that's okay. I play in a jazz band sometimes. Well, not play exactly. I sorta set up for these guys I know. But Judaism — I don't know nothin' about Judaism."

"You leave that to me. Why don't we just get together and talk. How's that?"

"I guess so. As long as you don't make me do anything I don't want to do, or serve me any more of that felafarful again."

"Sure, Bernie, no problem." The two Texans exchanged addresses and phone numbers, and set up a time to get together two days later.

MITCH HELLER spent the next forty-eight hours in intense thought. It was clear that his whole purpose in arriving in San Marcos was to reach out to Bernie Feldman. Every word he said to him would have to be measured, and every phrase rife with meaning about Jewish faith and practice. Never mind that his student would rather lasso a bronco than lay tefillin. Forget the fact that he was more interested in the rain dances of the local Apache tribe than in completing *hakafos* on Simchas Torah. Ignore the makeup of the individual who was just a dishwasher and not a brain surgeon or even a brain, for that matter. Rabbi Mitch Heller had entered the rabbinate to help his People, no matter who they were or where they were.

When they met on that fateful night, Mitch had done his homework. He was prepared for every scenario except the one Bernie sprang on him:

"I'm leaving Texas."

"You're what?"

"I'm splitting. I only ended up here 'cause I ran out of money hitchhiking out to LA. Now I've got enough, and it's time to hit the road. Only this time I'm gonna fly. No more hitchin' for me."

Crestfallen, Mitch could only stammer, "W-w-when?"

"In a couple a days. Nice gettin' to know you, and if there's ever anything I can do for you, just let me know."

All Mitch's hopes were going to be on that plane along with Bernie Feldman. "Could we get together before you leave?" the rabbi begged.

"I kinda doubt it. Still gotta lot to do. I appreciate your concern, though. Are you sure there isn't something I could do for you?"

MITCH EAGERLY CONTEMPLATED what would be an appropriate *mitzva*. "Elul is coming," he reminded himself. "Think! What about *shlugging kapporas*? Should I tell Bernie to take a live chicken and twirl it around his head? Nah, he'd never go for it. How about twenty-five hours without food and water on Yom Kippur? I'm not sure he's ready for that. There's got to be an easier *mitzva* to start with..."

"Look, Rabbi, I just came over to say goodbye, but I gotta go. If I don't start gettin' ready now, I'll miss my flight."

"Actually there is one thing you could do for me. Call it a personal favor."

"Okay, Rab, that's cool. Shoot."

"I want you to order a kosher meal for the flight out to the coast."

"But Rabbi, I'm not religious. I don't even know Hebrew. I don't know nothin'."

"That's why this is an excellent *mitzva* to begin with. The Sages say that you are what you eat, and kosher food is very healthful for the soul. Just do this and you're on your way, for '*mitzva gorreres mitzva*' — the fulfillment of one of God's commandments brings another one in its train."

"I'm not taking a train, man. I told ya, I'm flying."

"Regardless of your means of transportation, promise me you'll only eat a kosher meal."

"All right, I promise."

Mitch surrendered an exhausted smile as he put his arm around Bernie. "I'll be thinking about you every day. Please drop me a line when you get settled on the West Coast."

A HAZY TEXAS SUN hung high in the sky the day of Bernie's departure. He arrived at the airport wearing the uniform typical of his station in life: a backpack the size of a telephone booth, high-topped hiking boots, cut-off jeans, and little else, save a red bandana draped across his brow. His dish-pan hands clutched a pair of cowboy boots stuffed with memorabilia from the lone star state.

San Antonio Airport was mobbed and the check-in line for his flight spanned the length of the terminal. Bernie had hoped to take in a little brunch in the lounge since he had been up packing since 5:30 in the morning and hadn't had a chance to eat. By the time he arrived at the counter, however, they had already announced the final boarding call for his flight.

Bernie presented his ticket and the ground hostess quickly punched the requisite keys. "You're all set, Mr. Feldman: seat 23C, smoking, and I see a special meal has been ordered. Boarding is already under way so you'd better hurry to gate 3, over to the left, right after security. Enjoy your flight."

FLIGHT 211 from SAT to LAX was crowded but uneventful. Stewardess Tracy Mason, who was attending to the smoking section of the cabin, felt that the relative calm had something to do with the position of the moon and the stars. But then again, she thought everything had to do with the position of the moon and the stars. Since she spent so much of her life at 29,000 feet, it was only natural for astrology to rule her life.

Her spiritual forecast for that day, according to the paper's horoscope column, was to meet someone tall, dark, and handsome. This explains why she was concentrating more on whom she was serving than on what she was serving. Every passenger that day was awarded a tiny tray of what could optimistically be described as Chicken Kiev: a ragged strip of batter and bone soaked in an indeterminate broth and stranded among some wilted greens, alongside a piece of cinder block with red gumdrop icing.

A BEARDED but quite Presbyterian business-man from Austin motioned to the serving cart and Tracy graciously but inadvertently handed him a kosher meal and continued the search for her star. The Austinian wolfed down three-quarters of the Shrieber's corned beef sandwich and half the pickle before the flight attendant reached Bernie.

"What would you care to drink?" she asked as she placed the Russian delight on Bernie's tray table.

"Er, excuse me," Bernie said meekly, "but I ordered a kosher meal."

"Oh, I'm sorry," Tracy responded as she was trained. "I'll go check in the galley." A minute later she returned and asked, "Are you Mr. Feldman?" Bernie nodded his head. "I'm sorry, there must be some mistake. You're listed on the computer printout but I don't see the meal."

"No kosher meal?" Bernie implored, his stomach reverberating with the request.

"No, I'm very sorry," she apologized to the fellow she had already written off as a Taurus. "If we had a kosher meal, it must have been accidentally distributed to one of our normal, I mean, regular passengers."

Bernie was indignant, and hungry. "Aren't you supposed to be 'doing what you do best'?"

"We used to," Tracy explained like a schoolteacher addressing a young charge. "But we've changed our jingle. Now we're 'Something special in the air' and obviously this was messed up by the ground staff."

By now, Bernie's stomach was wailing the blues. "Why did I ever let myself get talked into ordering kosher food?" he scolded himself. "I'll just ask the stewardess to bring me a regular meal," he reasoned. "No one but her will know and obviously she doesn't care."

He was about to push the flight attendant button when his conscience began to nag him. "I did offer to do something for the guy and this was the only thing he asked for. He was nice enough not to make me learn or anything." With ravaged resolve he decided, "A promise is a promise."

FOR THE NEXT TWO HOURS, Bernie resorted to chain smoking to ward off his hunger. By the time he landed in Los Angeles, Bernie Feldman had only nicotine in his stomach and only one thing on his mind.

In consonance with his surroundings, he jet-propelled himself to the nearest restaurant in the terminal. Bernie quickly scanned the menu. It was typical. He had seen all the dishes in some form or other at Torres–Balalaika, and had probably washed off the residue of them all. He settled upon an order and then looked up at all the people chomping, chewing, swallowing, and drinking all around him. Suddenly the food didn't look appetizing and he left before the waitress returned.

"/%#*%!" he exclaimed and almost involuntarily stepped into a phone booth and looked up the listing of kosher restaurants. Technically he realized that he was already absolved of his commitment the moment he was off the plane, yet he felt compelled to honor the rabbi's parting wish.

Once he consumed the one kosher meal of his life, he would be free to resume his normal eating habits. Bernie found a couple of restaurants on Fairfax Avenue and dashed outside to hail a cab.

A FEW BLOCKS after El Coyote, the taxi pulled up in front of Steaks and Such, Fine Kosher Kuisine. Bernie hauled all his worldly possessions out of the cab, paid his fare, and then died a thousand deaths: the door was locked! In the window was a note that read, "Closed for the Nine Days."

"I can't believe it! I can't believe it!"

"Can't believe what?" a voice asked from behind him.

"I promised this weirdo rabbi in Texas that I would eat a kosher meal, and I've been trying all day. I'm starving and now this joint is closed!"

"Come with me. I'll take you to the best place in town, and it's strictly kosher."

"Thanks, buddy, you're a lifesaver. Where?"

"My house." And with that, Chaim Joseph, the owner of the steak house, bent down to scoop up Bernie's carry-on bag. Over supper Bernie started touting himself as any restaurateur's right-hand man, and by the time the meal was over he had landed a job as a dishwasher at Steaks and Such.

FOR THREE YEARS Bernie worked his way up, finally opening his own catering business. But by then, he was no longer Bernie Feldman, for the kid who had hitched through Texas had disappeared, never to be seen or heard from again. In his place came another member of an elite corps of Jews who discovered Judaism late in life.

It took a while, but eventually the young entrepreneur managed to keep his other promise to Rabbi Heller.

Dear Mitch,

I know you asked me to drop you a line when I got settled on the West

*Coast. Well, I arrived the same day I left,
but it took me quite some time to get
settled. Kashrus, Shabbos, building a
family—all this takes a while, you know.*

*But now I am truly settled, with a
commitment to God and to my wife and
two adorable children, all thanks to you!*

Gratefully,

Binyomin (nee Bernie) Feldman

Heard from: Rabbi Yitzchok Rosenberg

Top Flight

"**D**ECIDE!" the still, small voice inside Colonel Ernie Jacobs demanded. "Sit on the fence any longer and you'll lose the one p e r s o n you love!"

"I can't. I won't." Ernie Jacobs responded silently. "It's too much. I can't become someone I'm not, even for my son."

"That's a lie," the inner voice shot back. "You are a Jew and the time has come to live like one!"

"Colonel, is there anything wrong?" Rabbi Wallfish interrupted the internal debate.

"No, no," Ernie replied with a sad sigh.

"Then why were you shaking your head?" Colonel Jacobs' nine-year-old son Larry asked.

"Shaking my head? No, no, I was just thinking about what the rabbi was reading. Carry on, Chaplain."

"The purpose of tefillin is to bind one's intellectual and emotional faculties to God. Tefillin therefore serves as a bridge between the soul and its Creator. When a person puts on tefillin, he is enclosed in the mitzva. If a Jew never lays tefillin his whole life, his soul must descend to this world again and again until it fulfills this particular commandment, as well as any other *mitzvos* it may have missed."

"Wow!" Larry exclaimed. "I wonder how many times we've been through this up-and-down business."

Ernie Jacobs laughed at the thought of reincarnation. "I don't know. I'm having a hard enough time getting through this life!"

Seeing his father smiling, Larry turned to him enthusiastically. "Hey, Pop, I sure hope you enjoy learning this stuff as much as I do. After all, this is what it means to be Jewish."

Consternation clouded his father's face. "Larry," he said firmly, "I told you to stop bringing that up!"

COLONEL Ernie Jacobs was stationed at an air defense command base outside Colorado

Springs, Washington. The base's mission was as simple as it was deadly: Jacobs' group was to man the skies if and when the Cold War ever got hotter.

An expert in Soviet fighting tactics and equipment, a veteran of Korea, and a full colonel in the United States Air Force, Jacobs had a very important role to play in his country's defense.

As the father of a very bright boy whose mother had died when he was only seven, Jacobs had an equally important role to play in his son's upbringing. Right now, the two roles were engaged in a war in which there could only be one winner, and the first casualty was Colonel Ernie Jacobs' sense of identity.

Colonel Ernie Jacobs was the embodiment of the American dream. His parents had come to the New World at the end of World War II, after insufferable years as stateless Russians in China. Ernie was born while they were living in Shanghai, and no sooner had they immigrated to the U.S. than his parents drilled into him that he was "a real American."

As a real American, Ernie Jacobs had certain obligations to fulfill. He had to grow up in the right neighborhood, be clean-cut, and play Little League baseball. He had to attend the right school, have the right friends, and go to the right university. Consequently, he would marry the right girl and raise the right kind of family, a family that would carry on the tradition of the American way of life.

In short, Ernie's parents were determined to make their son a colorless, odorless, tasteless product of the American melting pot. Chances are, they would have succeeded if it hadn't been for the one person who mattered most in Ernie's life: his son.

I N MANY WAYS, Larry Jacobs was the spitting image of his father. Both were very traditional in their outlook and actions. Both had a highly developed sense of right and wrong. And both were capable of being quite stubborn when it came to matters of principle.

Larry Jacobs was the air force version of the typical army brat. Considering where his father's tours of duty had taken him it was to be expected. In the course of six years, he had slept in barracks at the Wright-Patterson, Langley, Edwards, and Hanscom air force bases, to mention but a few. At every base, the housing was the same, the food was the same, and the school was the same. With few friends and little else to do but read and think, a young boy grows up pretty fast. By the time Larry was nine, he felt and acted like he was twenty.

O NE DAY, not long after they'd arrived at Ent Air Force Base outside Colorado Springs, Colonel Ernie Jacobs and his son were invited to a Chanukah party arranged by the base chaplain. There, along with forty other Jewish soldiers, father and son ate *latkes* and listened to Israeli music.

"I know all about Chanukah," Larry told the rabbi. "I studied it when I was a kid."

"Oh, yes?" replied Rabbi Binyomin Wallfish, rather surprised at how this child felt his childhood was behind him.

"Yes. Mattathias and the rest of the oppressed Jews revolted and fought against the Greco-Syrian armies. The Jews won and freed their country." Larry crossed his arms with satisfaction.

"That's very interesting," the rabbi remarked. "But it sounds more like the Americans against the British than the Jews against the Greeks."

"What do you mean?"

"I mean that you've got your facts right, but your story wrong. Economically, politically, and socially, the Jews were relatively well off under the Greeks."

"Are you sure?" Larry uncrossed his arms and stepped closer.

"Of course. In fact, many of the Jews did not want to fight against the Greeks at all. They sought to be thoroughly acculturated so that they could live and look just like their Greek rulers."

"You're kidding!"

"No, I'm really not."

"What's going on?" Colonel Jacobs interrupted.

"We're just discussing the story of Chanukah," Rabbi Wallfish replied.

"The rabbi says the Jews had it good under the Greeks," Larry said, sounding like he still wasn't convinced.

"If the rabbi says so, it must be true."

"Would you mind if I gave your son a Chanukah present?" the rabbi asked.

"Why, that's very kind of you. I'm sure he'd appreciate it."

Rabbi Wallfish repaired to the back room and returned with two books: *A History of the Jewish*

Nation and *The Life of a Jew.*

"Please take these books as my personal gift," he told Larry. "I hope they make your Chanukah brighter." He then added, "May they bring you a lot of wisdom, and your father a lot of *nachas.*"

LARRY JACOBS read both books, and his world view exploded. "Hey, Pop, we're Jews. We're not Americans, we're Jews!"

"What are you talking about?" his father asked testily.

"I mean, I always thought we were like everyone else. But we're not. We didn't come over on the Mayflower. We didn't go exploring with Lewis and Clark. We didn't fight the Indians out west."

"So? What has that got to do with anything?" Colonel Jacobs demanded.

"Pop, listen to me. It says here Jews are supposed to be a 'holy nation.' We're supposed to be different."

"Let's get something straight, son," Ernie said, placing a heavy hand on Larry's shoulder. "We're no different from any other group of people. The next guy's no better than I am. And I'm no better than the next guy. The sooner you learn that lesson, the better off you're gonna be."

"Pop, I didn't say better, I said different. And we *are* different. Face it. You got passed over for a promotion a couple of times for being a Jew. You know it. I know it."

"You're wrong. If I got passed over, it was because someone else deserved the stripes more. Now let's drop this thing before we both lose our tempers. And if I were you, I wouldn't read any more of those books. They're only going to get you into trouble."

BUT ERNIE'S ATTEMPT to pull rank on his kid didn't work. With the tenacity of a military man, the not-so-raw recruit dug in his heels and continued the assault:

"Pop, remember when we were in Mobile? What about that?"

Ernie chuckled in spite of himself. As a wing commander, he had been in charge of a detachment in Mobile, Alabama. One November day he received a phone call.

"Commander?"

"How may I help you?" Ernie replied.

"My name is Mrs. Archibald White. I am looking for a dozen young airmen to join me for Thanksgiving dinner. Perhaps you could send some of your boys?"

"I believe that can be arranged, Mrs. White."

"Only one thing, Commander," the aging Southern belle drawled unctuously. "I have a personal request. Please do not send any Negroes, Catholics, or, Heaven forbid, Jews... I'm not prejudiced, of course. It's just that they wouldn't fit in. I'm sure you understand."

"Oh, yes," Colonel Ernie responded, "I understand *perfectly*."

"Good. Please have your driver take them to Clarendon Court — it's our own little plantation," Mrs. Archibald White giggled modestly. "Most people know where it is. And Commander, thank you."

"Oh, thank *you*, Mrs. White," the colonel replied sarcastically. As he hung up the phone, Colonel Jacobs called for his subordinate. "Sergeant?"

"Yes, Sir."

"How many men have we got in the brig?"

"Quite a few, Sir."

"I want you to pick out the twelve most hardened Asian and Hispanic prisoners — the ones with the glassiest eyes, the most outrageous tattoos, and the deepest scars — and send them all to this address Thanksgiving night."

"Yes, Sir."

A VITAL PART of American life for three-and-a-half centuries, Thanksgiving arrived on schedule in the dead of autumn. On this day of national tradition and personal imperative, 90% of America gathers around a table to stuff themselves with stuffing, gorge themselves on great gobbles of turkey, cram themselves with cranberry sauce, and ply themselves with pumpkin pie. Needless to say, each dish must be prepared, each condiment served, and each seasoning selected in accord with the immutable laws codified beside the brick ovens of pilgrim mothers, and not subject to modification by whim or culinary fashion. Each slab of turkey is a serving of tradition, each ladle of cranberry sauce an outpouring of American history, and each slice of pie a slice of life, love, and brotherhood — of thanksgiving and gratitude to the benevolent Lord who created all men free and equal.

For some people America's oldest and most

beloved holiday constitutes more than just a meal; it's a social event, a warm-up for the debutante balls and spectacular holiday soirees of December. Thanksgiving dinner at Mrs. Archibald White's was one of those must-attend events people wait for all year long. Everything from the flowers on the table to the perfume in the air had been chosen with the utmost care and her guest list was meticulously selected to enhance her reputation as "Mobile's hostess with the mostest."

That year, when the doorbell rang, Mrs. White regally sashayed to the front door in her frothy evening gown to answer it herself. As the big oak door swung open, she saw what appeared to be a gang of ugly, mean, nasty-looking toughs who were dressed up as airmen, but who couldn't possibly have been the ones she had "ordered" for dinner. There were Orientals, Hispanics, ethnic groups unto themselves, and subliterates, all fairly bursting with tattoos clearly visible from their unbuttoned shirts, and all appearing like criminals (which, coincidentally, they were).

At first Mrs. White was too stunned to do or say anything. So everyone just sort of stared at each other, waiting for someone to start the conversation. One airman belched, one gawked at her dress, while yet another stuck his head in the door and started to snoop around. When the lady of the house finally regained what was left of her composure, she managed to stutter, "E-e-excuse me, Sergeant. Are you sure you've come to the right house?"

"Is this Clarendon Court?"

"Yes, it is, b-b-but..."

"Then we've come to the right place."

"Perhaps your commander didn't understand me when I asked him to send me, uh, a *select* group of young men."

"Yes, Ma'am, he understood. He selected us."

"But I recall telling the colonel that I didn't want certain types, you know... Jews and the like. So there must be some mistake."

"Oh no, Ma'am. There couldn't be no mistake."

"How can you be so sure?"

"Because Colonel Jacobs *never* makes a mistake!"

LARRY RELAXED A FRACTION as he saw his father smile at the recollection. "See, Pop? The world is like that! Full of people who hate Jews. So we can't act like them!" He thumped the book in front of him for emphasis. "We gotta act like us."

"Look, I told you before to drop it. And I mean drop it!" Ernie Jacobs' voice was solid steel and determination, finely honed over twenty years of military service.

Larry knew better than to push his father too far. But, in his own way, he was just as determined.

FOR TWO WEEKS, all was quiet on the western front. Both Larry and his father went about their respective duties. Still, Larry made it a point to read as much as he could about Jews and Judaism. He raided the chapel library, snapping up everything that looked vaguely interesting to a mature nine-year-old: Ausabel's classic collection of Jewish folklore, an *I Remember Mama* cook-book, biographies, *Great Jewish Sports Heroes*, an English translation of *Ein Yaakov*, Philip Birnbaum's *Encyclopedia of Jewish Concepts*, and the list went on. With each book, Larry's commitment grew.

His father didn't notice the change taking place in his son until the day Larry began wearing a bright red yarmulke around the base.

"What are you doing?" Ernie bellowed. "This isn't a temple! It's a military installation. Do you want to embarrass me?"

"No," Larry replied, momentarily thrown by the intensity of his father's fury.

"Then stop this."

"I can't," Larry shrugged simply.

"What do you mean, you can't?"

"A Jew is supposed to fear no one, except the Creator. Wearing a yarmulke symbolizes that fact. I'll get one for you..."

"I don't care what it symbolizes! I told you to take it off around the base. You can wear it inside the house."

"Pop, please. I'm wearing it for a reason. Don't make me give it up."

Colonel Jacobs glared at his son; suddenly, an idea hit him. "Let's call the chaplain. I'm sure he can give you some sort of dispensation or some-thing."

Within seconds, Ernie had dialed Rabbi Wallfish and explained the situation. The rabbi was de-lighted that Larry had found Judaism so appealing, but he had never dreamed that he would come so far so fast.

The rabbi listened as both Ernie and Larry gave their sides of the yarmulke issue. Fortunately, this wasn't the rabbi's first such experience.

"I have a suggestion that should satisfy both of you. Larry, there's no reason for you to wear a yarmulke if it shames your father. After all, one of the cardinal *mitzvos* is honoring one's father."

"I knew you could explain it to him, Rabbi," Ernie said in a satisfied tone, and resumed breathing normally.

"On the other hand, Larry's right. A Jew's head should be covered..."

"See, Pop?" Larry said victoriously.

"Therefore, I recommend that Larry wear his yarmulke inside the house, and outside he can wear a hat. That way, everyone will be happy."

A ND SO IT WAS. Larry got a baseball cap emblazoned with the insignia of the LA Dodgers, and his father learned to accept the son of a USAF colonel who looked more like the son of a rabbi; that is, until the fateful breakfast when Larry said, "I can't eat this stuff. It's *treif*!"

"It's *what*!?" his father said, doing a double take.

"It's *treif*... unkosher. It'll foul up the whole system."

"What system?"

"Your internal system. You are what you eat; it says so explicitly in the book I'm reading. Just wait a second and I'll get it and show you..."

Colonel Jacobs had a hair-trigger temper, and Larry had just pulled it.

"Get out! Get out!" he yelled, lifting his son up by his shirt front. "This time, you've gone too far!"

"Pop, I'm sorry," Larry stammered. "I...I didn't mean to offend you."

"Out! Out, until you eat what we have!" And with that, the colonel bodily yanked Larry out of his chair, out of the room, and out of harm's way, until both father and son could cool down.

"What is this kid trying to do to me?" Ernie seethed.

EVER SINCE his wife had passed away, Jacobs had been both father *and* mother to his son. Now, he felt like a stranger. In his heart of hearts Larry understood that he was pushing his father to the limit, but he couldn't help himself. For the first time in his life, he felt he had some sense of roots, some idea of who and why he was, and a genuine sense of belonging.

Ernie Jacobs called the chaplain in a fit of paternal rage. "My kid won't eat," he yelled the second the phone was picked up.

Somewhat amused by a grown man shouting into the phone, Rabbi Wallfish's first inclination was to quip back, "Don't call me, call your pediatrician." Fortunately, he recognized that the frantic voice on the line belonged to a full colonel, and he responded more appropriately.

"I see. Let me talk to him."

Colonel Ernie had been a fighter pilot in Korea. He was a skilled flight instructor. An able administrator. Even a kind and patient father. But now he was feeling totally, absolutely, completely buffaloed. And the pièce de résistance was about to come...

Larry, Larry, come get on the phone."

"Please, don't call me that. I'm not Larry anymore."

"Whaaaat?"

"I want to be called by my Jewish name."

"You don't have a Jewish name!"

"Sure I do. I gave it to myself this morning. My name is Barook."

"Barook?"

"That's better!"

"Barook, Farouk, whatever your name is, it's gonna be mud if you don't get in here and on the phone!"

Barook (formerly Larry) walked in and picked up the receiver. "Shalom," he said.

"*Oy vey!* What have I created?" Rabbi Wallfish thought to himself. "Larry, listen to me..."

"My name is not Larry, it's Baroo..."

"Okay, okay, Baruch. 'Reb' Baruch, if you please. Do yourself a favor. Don't run before you can walk. Do you understand?"

"But I read that Jews have to eat kosher food."

"So who says your father's food is *treif*?"

"Bacon and eggs?"

"Uh, you have a point. But you've got to take things one step at a time. Let me talk to your father." Baruch Jacobs handed the phone back to Ernie.

"**L**ISTEN TO ME, Colonel. I have an idea that may help solve things. I would like you and your son to attend a weekly *shiur...*"

"A what?"

"I'm sorry. A 'briefing' on various topics of Jewish thought and practice. That way, I can control what he reads and you can monitor his progress..."

"I suppose I've got nothing to lose. I'll put Larry..."

"Barook, Pop!"

"Barook on the phone. You explain it to him."

THUS, father and son embarked on a bi-weekly spiritual journey at the home of Rabbi and Mrs. Wallfish. The colonel viewed the sessions as therapeutic, and each participant gained from the experience.

The chaplain commenced the series with a detailed explanation and analysis of the mitzva of honoring one's parents. The rabbi did not proceed until the concept was firmly fixed in Larry's mind (so much so that Ernie couldn't do a thing without his son offering to do it for him!). From there, Rabbi Wallfish began at the beginning, covering all the basics: belief in God, acceptance of the Torah, and the fulfillment of *mitzvos.*

Colonel Jacobs cherished the classes at the Wallfish home and ranked the time spent there as "quality minutes," where both father and son could amiably meet, discuss, and exchange ideas about their Jewish identity, heritage, and life. Rabbi Wallfish also enjoyed the sessions. Stationed where he was, he rarely had such bright and eager students who not only listened, but challenged him on every point. Woe to the rabbi if he wasn't adequately prepared! Baruch was no less enthusiastic, for the classes gave him a perspective and focus on all the books, pamphlets, and articles he had read.

FOR THE NEXT three months everything went well. Ernie and Baruch deepened their sense of Jewish life, and family harmony reigned. Until Uncle Sam placed a call. Suddenly the tenuous relationship between father and son, rabbi and students, and colonel and superior officers was placed in jeopardy. The order from the Pentagon had arrived: Colonel Ernest F. Jacobs was to report to Washington, D.C., at once.

"Pop, you can't let them transfer you! Not after all this. You can't!"

"Larry, I mean, Barook, I don't know what they want. But whatever it is, I am a soldier and that means I have to follow my orders. It's not that different from what we've been learning in class. A Jew has to follow orders, too."

"Promise me they won't ship us off to some hick town or foreign country."

"I can't promise anything. But we always knew I'd have to transfer. Everyone has to at some time or other, even Rabbi Wallfish. Life in the military is a transient existence. But let's not worry about it until I get back. Okay?"

"Okay, but..."

"Please, no 'buts.' I'll be back in two days. In the meantime, I've made arrangements for you to stay with Rabbi Wallfish. Just don't drive him crazy with your questions."

THE NEXT AFTERNOON, Colonel Ernie Jacobs found himself straightening his uniform and taking a very deep breath before entering the office of General Maxwell Mays.

As a twenty-year veteran of the United States Air Force, Jacobs was used to briefings and debriefings. Nonetheless he was nervous about this meeting, and for good reason. Rumor had it that the general wanted to assign Colonel Ernie Jacobs the kind of post most top air force men only dream about — command of an air defense command base.

"Colonel Jacobs reporting, Sir."

"At ease, Colonel. Please have a seat."

"Thank you, Sir."

"Jacobs, as you know, you've been recommended for a position as a command base officer. From everything in your records, the job sounds like it would be a natural for you."

"Thank you, Sir." Jacobs swallowed. "What command did you have in mind?"

"The hottest one we've got."

Another swallow. "You mean, Elmendorf?"

"That's right. The air base closest to the Reds.

It's got the best birds, the best men, and the best equipment. It's the career opportunity of a lifetime. Spend two years there, and the next step is Washington, on my staff. Believe me, I know some guys who would give their right arm for this assignment. What do you say?"

"Are you kidding? Why, of course..." Suddenly, the voice of a lonely, stubborn nine-year-old burst into his ear: "Promise me..."

The colonel tried to shake the thought out of his head. "Excuse me, Sir, must I give you my answer now?"

"Well, if you don't think you're up to the post..."

Jacobs shifted awkwardly in his leather armchair. "It's not that, Sir. It's just that I've got a son, and, well, he's very interested in being around kids with his, uh, background."

"He'll just have to get used to being without them. I'm sure he'll make new friends in Elmendorf. Surely you're not thinking of giving up this assignment just because he might miss his playmates?"

"No, Sir. Of course not. But I would like to have a few days to talk it over with him..."

"Colonel, I'll give you seventy-two hours. But if I were in your position, this decision wouldn't take me seventy-two seconds."

ALL THE WAY back to Colorado Springs, Colonel Jacobs went over and over the next seventy-two hours in his mind. On the one hand, this assignment would be a very large and very obvious feather in his cap, a sign to everyone (even his deceased parents) that he had succeeded in life. But more important, it was the challenge of his career, and an opportunity to serve his country in a monumental way.

On the other hand, he dreaded having to face his son. Under Rabbi Wallfish's tutelage, not only had Baruch blossomed, but so had their relationship.

Aside from the familial considerations, Ernie had to admit that he was attracted to the way Judaism elevated the mundane. It appealed to the pilot in him. As someone accustomed to looking at the world from 39,000 feet, he sensed that there was a lot more to life than what appeared to be taking place below.

Still, this assignment was a once-in-a-lifetime chance. Ernie's brain felt like it was engaged in a Ping-Pong tournament. Every argument had a counterargument. "Sure the assignment looks good, but you know from experience that nothing is ever as good as it looks. The base is probably old, the men are probably bored, and the operational status is never as effective as it's made out to be. The place is probably a can of worms and they want you to have the privilege of opening it. Here you know who's who and what's what." Such reasoning was a valiant attempt, but it crumbled under attack.

"That's the challenge. And you can handle it. That's what you've been doing here. And that's what you can do there, only this time in a job where *you* get the glory, not someone else..."

WHEN ERNIE arrived back at the base, Baruch was waiting. Without even a "hello" or "welcome back," he blurted out, "What's the assignment?"

The colonel couldn't look his son directly in the face. "They want me to go to Alaska."

"Alaska?! You can't. There's nothing there. No rabbis. No kosher food. No *latkes*. No nothing!"

"I know. But this assignment is important for my career, and for our country."

"Our country is Israel." Baruch looked at his father uncomprehendingly. "That's where we belong."

"Don't get started. Look, I didn't give General Mays my answer yet."

"Then you haven't made up your mind?"

"No, not yet." Baruch breathed a sigh of relief. "Do we have a class tonight?"

"Yes."

"Then let's go. Right now, I'd rather learn than think."

RABBI Wallfish decided to devote the night's class to the mitzva of tefillin. Although Baruch's bar mitzva was several years off, the chaplain reasoned that it wasn't too early to introduce the colonel to the concept. Little did Rabbi Wallfish realize that when the time for celebrating the bar mitzva finally came, it might entail the importation of a *minyan* to Alaska.

Meanwhile, Colonel Jacobs' head was not in his studies; it was too busy shuttling between Washington and Alaska. He had to choose between career and family. He wished there were a way out. Suddenly a light bulb went on in his head.

"Rabbi," the colonel interrupted the class, "may I have a word with you privately?"

"Certainly," Rabbi Wallfish replied.

For the next half hour the colonel and the chaplain sequestered themselves in the rabbi's private office. When they emerged, Ernie looked relieved.

"Pop, did you make a decision?"

"I'll inform you tomorrow night."

THE NEXT DAY, Colonel Jacobs placed a phone call to Washington. He begged General Mays' indulgence and related everything that had transpired in his personal life since his wife had passed away two years earlier. After detailing his delicate relationship with his son, he made a series of requests, all of which General Mays agreed to.

All day long Baruch waited with keen anticipation for his father to come home. As soon as he heard the squeel of the jeep tires, he leaped to his feet, hoping that his anxiety had come to an end. Eventually a staff car pulled up to their house and Colonel Jacobs emerged from the passenger seat.

Baruch darted out of the house, still wearing a yarmulke. "Well, Pop? Did you tell them to forget it?"

"Let's go inside first," Ernie replied, placing a fatherly arm around his son and leading him indoors.

Inside their home, Ernie sat down, looked his son squarely in the eye, and said, "Baruch, I've always tried to have your best interests at heart. But at the same time, this assignment is a very special one."

"So?"

"So I've decided to take it."

Larry was visibly deflated. "But what about us? How are we going to keep learning?"

"That's taken care of."

"What do you mean?"

"I mean, I've asked Rabbi Wallfish to come along!"

"WHEN a student is exiled, his teacher enters into exile with him," relates the Talmud. True to tradition, Rabbi Wallfish accepted the transfer. The Jacobs' learning continued and so did their religious commitment, and Ernie earned the highest commendation: his son's respect. By the end of Colonel Jacobs' tour of duty, Baruch celebrated his bar mitzva. He had become a man, and so had his father.

Heard from: Mrs. Edith Weissman

Wrench
of the
Heart

IN THE SAME WAY that shtetl peddlers depended upon their horses and carts, Shimon Morgenthal needed his car. Commuting salespeople take planes, trains, and cabs, but Morgenthal was only a travelling salesman. He eked out his commissions partly by taking orders, but mostly by schlepping in his station wagon a variety of upholstery supplies that were likely to be in demand — if the word "demand" can be applied to the no-longer-in-vogue upholstery supply business. By driving around with bales of cotton wadding, rolls of webbing, chair springs, bolts of fabric, and boxes of tacks, he could meet small, on-the-spot orders immediately or deliver at least some of an order while writing up the rest.

In this way, he serviced his "territory": upstate, the Island, Jersey, and southern Connecticut. Wherever a lone upholstery shop existed, Morgenthal made his calls, wrote up his orders, and commiserated over the prevailing consumerism that had given rise to disposable furniture, which home owners replaced every few years instead of re-upholstering.

O VER THE YEARS a succession of vehicles of varying description — and in varying condition — helped carry Morgenthal's stock. His latest was a once-proud Ford Falcon, now crestfallen and bereft of its plumage. Its chrome trim and gleaming hubcaps were not even memories, and a wooden bumper partially replaced the metal one that had originally spanned its back. Rust completely eclipsed each wheelwell and a series of minor accidents had rearranged both rear doors. The pseudo-Leatherette upholstery, once stitched in intricate contours, was now a series of unconnected strips bursting at the seams. Foam and springs peeked out from beneath like the bones of a beggar under tattered rags. As the shoemaker's children go barefoot, so were the car seats of this travelling upholstery salesman left to benign neglect.

The wagon's decrepit features hardly mattered to the Morgenthals, especially the seven smaller ones. Having a car altogether was enough to insure vehicular pride. The family was mobile at least horizontally, if not upwardly, and Shimon did keep the little ones in shoes. The old Falcon was pressed into service not only on weekdays — to carry merchandise — but on idyllic Sundays, when it bounced the family out of the city to breathe the country air of such exotic locales as Bloomsberg or Brewster. On these long outings Morgenthal would glow with the satisfaction of giving his wife a well-deserved respite from her bricked-in world of four tiny rooms. These "luxurious" excursions were the weekday equivalent of a Shabbos treat. They offered the numbing pleasure of nine persons of varying size wedged into one car and sharing the scenery as it spun by their grimy windows.

Even with one day of rest, driving all day, six days a week takes its toll on a motorist — and not just in terms of making change on the turnpike. Unable to maintain his car as he should yet unable to survive without it, nothing produced such a cold cramp in Shimon's stomach as his wagon making the wrong noises, or not making the right ones. Some people drive with their eyes open; Morgenthal drove with his ears and nose equally engaged, alerted to sound and sniff out any signs of imminent disaster for his fragile Falcon.

L ITTLE WONDER that the worst of all possible scenarios assaulted all three senses: the acrid smell of something burning, the ominous hiss of evaporating liquid, and the dark gray plume of steam. The inhabitants of the nearest service garage all stopped in the middle of their appointed rounds to watch poor Morgenthal limp, as if on square tires, into view.

They had already heard him coming. The minute the wounded Falcon lurched onto their turf, Morgenthal envisioned dollars he did not have flying out of his pocket. The garage attendants shared this vision, only they pictured those dollars arcing and stacking into their cash register.

Not that the men of the Seventh Avenue Service Center did not plan to work for their money. Like surgeons conferring on a critical-condition case, they huddled over the Falcon's opened hood, peering, pointing, probing, pondering, and finally quietly shaking their heads and coming away with a common prognosis.

The patient would require the most deliberate and delicate of mechanical manipulations, involving skilled men and maneuvers, state-of-the-art equipment and expertise, and myriad additives and fluids — all costing no less than $142.50 with parts and labor. That was, of course, barring unforeseen complications, for with a victim of such advanced age there could be no guaranteed cure.

Unable to tear himself away from the grisly sight of his wounded wagon, and grateful not to be banished to a typical customer waiting room replete with dog-eared *Car and Driver* magazines and abandoned cups of coffee polluted by floating orbs of congealed grease, Morgenthal watched the ministrations of the men in the dark green jumpsuits. The mechanics didn't ordinarily perform before an audience, but they were certainly up to providing some drama for this obviously unsuspecting Jew. Only the slowest movements could apparently be risked (at $39.00 an hour), as if the car's condition bordered not just on the terminal but on the explosive.

After *davening mincha* and reciting some *tehillim* selected for just such an occasion, Morgenthal braced himself as a massive, lethal-looking power tool was lowered into the bowels of the station wagon. There it *shuckled* back and forth with deliberate rhythm until its uneasy extraction.

The patient would live. But like the recipient of a triple bypass or a pacemaker implant, the vehicle would be an eternal outpatient requiring regular observation and maintenance. Sent on his way with strict warnings to return no less than once every two months for perpetual therapy (tightenings) at only $39.95 a session, Morgenthal became anxious every time his Falcon spread its clipped wings and flew too far from its new nest: the Seventh Avenue Service Center.

HIS ROUTE was his route, however, and the odometer spun on, even after the cash-strapped family man had given up his Sundays out. Tightenings came and went, and being a man who at least knew a bolster from a butterfly spring, Morgenthal eventually decided to take on the dragon directly, buying one of those enormous wrenches and performing the tightenings himself.

He duly purchased the wrench, an imposing Allenhead of silvered magnitude, which remained at the ready in the back of the car. Accessible was another story. Emboldened by the acquisition, the Morgenthals bravely took to the road to transport the oldest four children to summer camp.

The wagon's cargo area was piled high with a summer's supply of clothes, washing cups, *siddurim,* and other amorphous baggage in several battered suitcases and boxes, along with sacks of fruit and nosh, diapers, wipes, changes of clothing, pillows, thermoses, and the ubiquitous plastic *sheitel* box for the non-campers. Rearview mirror visibility was at a premium.

No question, then, that when steam began to swirl and gasp from beneath the hood, it seemed eminently easier to straggle into a service station near Lake Sheldrake than to unpack the entire back of the wagon in order to reach the tightening tool tucked well under the cargo floor.

WHEN IT HAPPENED AGAIN, with a full consignment of heavy chair springs en route to a shop near Peekskill, expediency once again dictated letting someone else deal with the front end of the car rather than having to shift the hundreds of pounds of intransigent steel at the back.

Truth to tell, Morgenthal, hardly mechanical by nature or knowledge, had sufficient fear of the steamy, serpentine insides of his car's engine to be reluctant, if not petrified, to actually take up the cudgel, or in this case the mighty wrench, and go forth into the fray. What can seem so routine in the hands of the experienced can loom as an awesome undertaking in the hands of the awkward. Reason and economics may encourage self-reliance, but that resolve can evaporate rapidly when the chips are down and the hood is up.

When unquestionable necessity comes knocking, however, that was something else. A totally deserted road and no help within miles might indeed have forced Morgenthal to finally wield his intimidating power wrench. So it was that returning home safely each night gave him cause to sigh with relief.

THEN, one night, after clattering home with only a few rolls of webbing and boxes of tacks sliding balefully back and forth in the cargo space, he emerged from what passed for his car to find the front door congested with frantic children. "Tatie, Tatie!" they shrieked, "come quick! Basya's hand is stuck. Come! Come!"

He had only to see his wife's panic-stricken eyes and hear the child's hysterical, shuddering sobs to confirm his deepest fears. Little Basya's hand had been thrust into the meat grinder, her fingers wedged between the twists of the shaft.

"Don't turn the handle!" a hundred voices seemed to scream. And with good reason. Each turn would bring the fingers inexorably closer to the deadly blades.

"The doctor said to get her hand out and bring her right over!" his wife half-panted, half-sobbed, her fright palpable.

But how to extricate the child whose frightened fidgeting was jeopardizing every finger of her hand? How to dismantle the grinder? How to take apart the components and free the tiny eighteen-month-old fingers?

"RIBBONO SHEL OLAM, show me what to do," Morgenthal prayed. And suddenly, in the pandemonium of the moment, calm flowed into his heart. At the bottom end of the grinder his fingers felt a strangely shaped nut. Maybe with that off, the shaft would come loose. But how could he remove it? Pliers would never budge such a nut. Then it hit him.

The wrench!

In seconds he was out the door and rummaging in the back of the wagon. Seizing the wrench, he moved so fast that some of the children were still rushing out to follow him as he raced back in, nearly colliding with some half a dozen bodies.

His wife grasped the chubby little arm to keep it still and taut; one false move could spell disaster. Morgenthal tightened the wrench around the nut and slowly began to increase pressure. All breathing seemed to cease. Even Basya forgot to whimper. Would the nut come loose? Would the shaft stay still under the strain, or would it start to turn? Here was the tool that destiny had forced into his hands. Would the wrench hold true?

Morgenthal gripped the instrument with even greater determination and, with beads of perspiration now dotting his forehead, applied more pressure. The nut squeaked and began to loosen, rotating with increasing ease until it finally fell to the floor. The shaft itself was now free to be eased up gently, along with little Basya's hand. Cries of "*Baruch Hashem! Baruch Hashem!*" filled the air.

In a true twist of fate, the dreaded wrench had done its work.

Heard from: Rabbi Shlomo Moddel

A Tale
of Two Cities

H UNGARY is a land of rolling plains and ominous mountains. About the size of Indiana, it has twice the population and over than five times the history. Much of that history has been written and rewritten to suit the last country to conquer it.

Major protagonists in Hungary's evolving saga were the Jewish communities of Budapest, Debrecen, Szget, and hundreds of other *kehilos*, towns, and villages. Like many Hungarians, most Jews were poor people who lived off whatever the Hand of Heaven sent their way.

One of them was Moshe Adler.

A shoemaker by trade, Moshe earned his living making and repairing boots for people who usually couldn't afford them. He often joked that the only things that lasted longer than his shoes were his invoices.

Moshe and Miriam Adler lived in the town where he grew up, Vac, about twenty kilometers north of Budapest on the Danube River. During the 1930s Vac boasted about 18,000 people. No one knows how many were Jews. Tear-stained pages of Jewish history had taught them that the best way to keep out of trouble was to keep out of sight.

Still, the Jewish community was active, if not conspicuous. There were six shuls, one *mikva* (not counting the Danube), and even a rabbinical court.

Moshe Adler's store was actually the front of his house. In the rear lived the eight Adlers. But to be accurate, the town of Vac was the real home of the Adler family. They were raised and educated there; to go anywhere else was unthinkable. It would have been like turning their back on an old family custom. And Moshe Adler took his custom — and his customers — very seriously:

"Yes, Mrs. Rabinowitz, I will be happy to repair these shoes for the twenty-sixth time. I understand that you only bought them nineteen years ago. But you should know, not even the cow whose hide they were made from lasted that long!"

Miriam contributed to the family budget by sewing for the ladies in town. She had a knack for turning a Shabbos dress into something special enough for a wedding, then turning the wedding gown into a dress fit for Yom Tov. Often the alteration amounted to no more than a piece of ribbon here, a few buttons there. In many ways, her work was like her husband's. They were both adept at "spinning straw into gold," or at least ersatz wool.

MOSHE AND MIRIAM Adler had one pet mitzva, one particular custom that they never failed to observe. Whenever someone left town, the Adlers would arrange a farewell party in his honor. Actually, a *seudas predah* is not just a goodbye party. It's more of a "goodbye and good luck" party.

As a matter of fact, the tradition (even though Moshe and Miriam didn't know it) began with the holiday of Shemini Atzeres. According to the Midrash, after seven days of intense communion with His beloved People on Sukkos, God begged the Jews to maintain the festival for one more day — Shemini Atzeres —because their parting was so difficult for Him.

In any event, a *seudas predah* hosted by Moshe and Miriam Adler was not just a social event. It represented a chance for the community to come together for a *simcha* (albeit a bittersweet one). A chance to exchange old stories and live new ones. A chance to be aware of the Lord's ever-vigilant Providence.

THE ADLERS' custom of making a *seudas predah* began with the departure of a *melamed*, Reb Gedalia Cracower. Reb Gedalia was on his way from Cracow to Budapest when he took a temporary job in Vac. "I will only stay for the winter, just long enough for you to find a really qualified teacher," he told his students' parents. Winter turned to spring, spring to summer, and before he knew it, seventeen years had passed. By then, some of Reb Gedalia's original students were raising families of their own. When the *melamed* finally packed his bags, Moshe and Miriam decided they couldn't just let him leave. So they made their first *seudas predah*. It was held at the old "Strasse" shul. Inside, there was honey cake, schnapps, fish, and treats for the children. There were also speeches, as each parent and friend stepped forward to speak the words that had been inscribed on his heart. Reb Gedalia tried to thank the townspeople for their unceasing support. But instead of speaking, he simply cried.

That did it. As if on cue, all the women in the crowded room began to weep. Then all the children. And finally, the men. Pretty soon, there wasn't a dry eye in the place. People wailed and bawled, and a flood of tears flowed forth like spring on the Danube.

"*Rabbosai*! *Rabbosai*!" Moshe's voice cracked as he fought to control his emotions. "This is how we celebrate a *simcha*? Thank God, we have plenty of things to be unhappy about. But this shouldn't be one of them!"

A few people sniffled and giggled at the same time.

"According to our Sages," Moshe continued, "the souls of the Jewish people are always together, even when their bodies are apart So why are we upset? Let's make a *l'chaim*. Two *l'chaims*: one for Reb Gedalia and one for us!"

Mrs. Sophie Gittleman undoubtedly spoke for all the attendees when she later remarked, with a twinkle in her eye, "*Oy*! Was that a *simcha*!"

That was the town's first *seudas predah*. But not the last. There were many such gatherings, each more *heimish* and heartwarming than the last. There was the *seudah* for Reb Yaakov Rosenthal the tailor, when he fulfilled his lifelong dream of moving to Eretz Yisrael. There was the *seudah* for Rebbetzin Engel, who, when her husband passed on, left to live with her sister in Debrecen. However, the most talked-about *seudas predah* Miriam and Moshe ever made was the one for their butcher, Yitzchak Adler.

BESIDES their last name, Moshe and Yitzchak Adler had nothing in common. Moshe was an upbeat extrovert with a quick smile and an even quicker wit. He had about two hundred favorite jokes and even though he exhausted his entire repertoire week after week, each rendition was interrupted by peals of his audience's unaffected laughter.

Yitzchak Adler's humor vacillated between biting cynicism and caustic sarcasm. He was particularly fond of the verse in the Torah in which the Children of Israel complain to Moses, "Because there weren't enough graves in Egypt, is that why you brought us out?" He admired their angle and would editorialize, "Those were rebels with a cause."

Yitzchak was much older than Moshe. His children were grown, and he was a widower of fourteen years. Fortunately, his profession as a butcher kept him both solvent and stable. Carving and stabbing slabs of meat had a therapeutic effect upon the cantankerous curmudgeon.

One fateful day, as portent poisoned the air and snow-laced clouds battled a pale sun struggling to break free, the lives of Yitzchak Adler and his name-sakes were changed forever.

RABBI AARON ZIGFRIED, the Rav of Vac, entered Yitzchak's shop at eleven in the morning. The rabbi strode ahead of the customers waiting to be served and asked Yitzchak to come with him to the back of the store for a moment. Yitzchak did not like the idea of abandoning his patrons, but he followed the rabbi nonetheless.

"Yitzchak," Rav Zigfried spoke gently, "the *Vaad Harabbanim* held a meeting last night."

Some basic instinct put Yitzchak on his guard. "So?"

"As you know, there are three butcher shops in and around Vac. We've decided to set up a *Vaad Hakashrus* to supervise them. Starting on *rosh chodesh*, we want every place to have a *mashgiach timidi*, including yours."

"You can't be serious!" Adler gasped. "My father was a butcher. And my father's father before him. Not once in three generations of Adlers has there ever been a *shailah*! If you put a pair of eyes over my shoulder, people will say it's because I need it."

"I'll make sure they understand."

"Understand? *You* don't understand. There isn't enough money in my business to feed myself, much less a hired *mashgiach*. If you want to provide someone with a *parnassa*, let him work for somebody else."

"That's not the point," Rabbi Zigfried interrupted.

"It *is* the point," Yitzchak countered. "Half the time, I end up eating scraps no one else would buy! If I pay a *mashgiach*, I'm going to have to raise my prices. If I raise my prices, I'll lose whatever business I have. Then you'll have two *Yiddin* looking for a job, not just one!"

"Yitzchak. Listen to me," the rabbi said, trying to sound soothing. "We're doing this not because of you, but because of the other butchers. Some of them need supervision..."

"So go supervise them. Who's stopping you?"

"No one wants to let us in unless everyone agrees to."

"And if I refuse?"

"We'll go ahead and organize anyway. If we succeed, we'll let everyone know that you're not under our supervision."

Yitzchak winced at the thought of how such innuendo would besmirch the good Adler name.

"Please, just go along with us," Rabbi Zigfried cajoled. "You'll see that it will work. Think about it."

But the butcher would not be bullied. "There's nothing to think about. Not one Adler has ever had a *mashgiach*, and I'm not going to be the first!"

"Is that your final decision?"

Yitzchak stared at the rabbi for several maddeningly long seconds. "I believe I've made my position rather clear," he growled. "Now if you don't mind, I have several customers to wait on."

The rabbi sadly turned and left.

BEFORE LONG, word of Yitzchak Adler's firm stance spread. When the other butchers heard about it, they met to discuss the situation. None of them was even close to being wealthy. Yet, being young and flexible, they all saw the *Vaad* as a way to get more customers... especially if it meant there would eventually be one less competitor in town.

And so, to make a painfully protracted story mercifully short, that's exactly what happened. Every butcher proudly displayed his certificate of affiliation with the new *Vaad Hakashrus*, except Yitzchak Adler.

"Things will get better," Miriam Adler would say to her namesake. She made it a point to continue her patronage, even though her friends and neighbors had long since taken their business elsewhere.

"I'll be happy if they don't get worse," Yitzchak responded dryly.

In her inimitably sweet way, Miriam tried to calm her butcher's growing anxiety. "Who knows? Maybe God has big plans for you."

"Yes, obviously He was looking for a renegade carnivore to become Hungary's first vegetarian!"

AFTER SIX AGONIZING MONTHS, there wasn't even a bone to be thrown at Yitzchak Adler. He was unmistakably and irrevocably out of business. By this time, he wasn't even upset. He was resigned and thoroughly defeated. In his heart of hearts, he understood that even if he recanted and submitted to the *Vaad Hakashrus*' watchful eyes his customers would never trust him again. "Well, I can always begin a new career as a *mashgiach*," he told Mrs. Adler ruefully.

Feeling understandably unwelcome in Vac, Yitzchak Adler decided to try his luck — if indeed he still had any — in America. He had relatives there, and after all, wasn't it time he tested out the age-old axiom *meshaneh makom, meshaneh mazel*, change your spot, change your lot?

When news of her butcher's imminent departure reached Miriam Adler, she resolved to make a *seudas predah* for him. Her husband, however, had other ideas. "Absolutely not," he declared. "He caused his own failure. In fact, if Yitzchak Adler had his way, there would be no *Vaad*, no *mashgichim*, and no consistent standard of *kashrus* in Vac. In my book, he's wrong."

"But he's not a bad person!" Miriam pleaded. "He still *davens*. He still wears a yarmulke and *tzitzis*. He's still the same butcher we used for twenty years. And besides, if we don't have a *seudah*, he'll be disgraced!"

Moshe wasn't convinced. "Look, I'm sure Rabbi Zigfried won't come to any *seudas predah* held for Yitzchak Adler. And if he won't come, then we shouldn't have it!"

"I'll talk to the rabbi, and I expect you to go along with his ruling."

Moshe stared at his wife. He was aware of the Talmudic insight that women were blessed with "*bina yesaira*," an extra measure of understanding and intuition. Still...

"Why should we go out of our way for him?" he asked.

"Because if we go out of our way for everyone else he's no different."

At last Moshe Adler shrugged his shoulders and sighed. For better or for worse, the shoemaker had been shoehorned into his wife's party plans.

T HE *SEUDAS PREDAH* was scheduled to take place in two weeks. For the next fourteen days, the town was buzzing. Would the *rav* come or wouldn't he? Should the Adlers hold the *seudah* or shouldn't they? No one was aware of the Adlers' consultation with the rabbi and the talk went on and on.

Finally, the big day came. Moshe forced himself to be cheerful. "Most people want to leave Vac for Israel, the Land of Milk and Honey. But Reb Yitzchak is going to America, the Land of Gold and Money!"

That broke the ice. But it was Rav Aaron Zigfried who melted it. "I came here to honor a good friend, a God-fearing Jew, and a fine butcher, Reb Yitzchak Adler. Reb Yitzchak comes from three generations of *shochtim*. Each set the standard of piety in Vac. And that includes Reb Yitzchak. For that, our entire town owes him our deepest and most sincere thanks..."

When Rav Zigfried finished speaking, it was Reb Yitzchak's turn. "The Torah calls the Jews a stiff-necked people. I myself never realized how true that statement was until just recently."

The room burst into warm laughter.

"However, let me say that I bear no grudge against Rabbi Zigfried or anyone else for what happened. He did what his position called for. And, I guess, as the last of the line of Adler butchers, so did I. But I just want to let you all know that I'll miss you, and I'll think of Vac often, and..."

"Cut the baloney!" someone yelled out from the back amid more laughter.

"That's exactly what I'm going to do in America!" Yitzchak shot back, grinning.

And so he did. In a quirk of *Hashgacha* somewhere between a footnote in history and a sizable irony, Yitzchak Adler arrived at Ellis Island in 1938, and was soon swallowed up among the thousands of other faceless, nameless refugees. For all the villagers of Vac knew, he had sailed off the edge of the earth.

MOSHE AND MIRIAM ADLER and their co-religionists continued to live (in a manner of speaking) in the town Yitzchak Adler had left. It wasn't easy for a Hungarian, a Magyar, and least of all a Jew to reside in a country in alliance with Nazi Germany. In 1941, Hungary joined Germany in its Russian invasion. But facing mounting casualties on the Russian front, and fearful of his country's archenemy, Rumania, Prime Minister Miklos Kallay tried to withdraw from the conflict as much as possible, which earned him nothing but Germany's distrust. Everyone knew that it was only a matter of time before voracious Germany would swallow Hungary whole. In anticipation, people were fleeing Vac. Rumor had it that they were being forced out, but that rumor could not be verified, for everyone was too frightened to risk speaking to one another.

Moshe Adler's enterprise lost its sole and its soul. There was a leather shortage. A cloth shortage. A copper rivet shortage. And a customer shortage.

To the Adlers it was clear that the time had come to leave, although their clarity of perception did nothing to secure their escape. Moshe turned to his wife for advice but all she could offer was faith.

"God will help. You'll see," she said bravely. But the worry lines on her pale face revealed more concern than confidence.

ONE DAY, as Miriam was making her way back home with what little groceries were still available, she encountered her friend Goldie Weinstock. A warm, energetic woman with a big laugh and a bigger heart, Goldie had been a regular at the Adlers' famous *seudos*, back when there was something to celebrate. She and Miriam had spent hours together in the Adlers' tiny, makeshift kitchen, crying over their onions as they reminisced about whoever they were soon to bid farewell. But today, the gregarious Goldie had no time to socialize.

"Do you have any money?" she asked urgently. "I'll sell you these silver candlesticks; they were my mother's."

From out of a worn winter coat, Goldie removed two huge, ornate candlesticks, buffing them lovingly with her tattered sleeve. They were clearly priceless.

"Goldie, why?" Miriam asked incredulously. After all, no one was starving... yet.

"I have a chance to go to New York. My brother's there. He will sign the papers if I can pay my way. Miriam, I must leave. Please, can you help me?"

"Goldie, I'll do what I can. But I could never pay you what they're worth."

"Just enough to cover the boat ticket. That's all I ask." Goldie's eyes were wide with fear.

MIRIAM HURRIED HOME and related the story to her husband. Moshe was known for his kindness and generosity and for once his wife intended to exploit it. But from Moshe's perspective, this was too much; her latest benevolent impulse had surpassed the realm of *chessed* and entered the realm of masochism.

"Miriam," he asserted in a stern voice, "we have managed to put away a little money. That's all we have left. If we give it to Goldie, what will become of us?"

"As I told you, the Lord will help. Any government — elected, self-appointed, conquering, or occupying — will need skilled craftsmen. You have a skill. I have a skill. But poor Goldie has nothing but a pair of candlesticks she inherited from her mother. Besides," Miriam added with a note of pragmatism, "we don't have enough for our family. But we do have enough for her."

Swayed by his wife's common sense and uncommon compassion, Moshe shuffled to the corner of the hallway, discreetly lifted up a loose board, gingerly fished for what few coins lay underneath, and silently handed them to his wife.

Later that night, Mrs. Adler exchanged gold for silver.

"Oh, Miriam, how can I ever thank you?" Clutching the four worn coins in her hopeful hand, Goldie embraced her friend and their tears mingled.

"There is a way," Miriam replied softly but with sudden inspiration. "I want you to send us a phone book from New York."

"A phone book? What for?"

"Please, just promise me you'll do it the very first thing!"

"If I can, of course..."

"No 'if's. You must!" Miriam extricated herself from Goldie Weinstock's grateful arms and enveloped her in a silent stare.

Goldie nodded her head resolutely.

THREE-AND-A-HALF MONTHS after Goldie departed for safety, Miriam received a large package that had obviously been opened and resealed several times before it reached her hands. Miriam's heart sank. Even before examining the return address she knew who had sent it. She had asked for a telephone book and Goldie had given her solemn word. But overwhelmed by the materialism of the New World, the ex-Vacite had sent her a gift instead. With trembling fingers, Miriam broke open the package and found it filled with useless little trinkets, probably scavenged from the garbage, voluminously wrapped in pages of the New York directory. To make sure the authorities wouldn't be suspicious, she had wisely used the pages of the phone book as stuffing and padding.

All night, Miriam set about arranging the "A" pages alphabetically. Her husband was flabbergasted. "Miriam," he said, in a tone that he hoped would steer her back to sanity, "I realize that you are out of work and so am I, but there has got to be something more productive for us to do, even at this hour of the morning."

Oblivious to her husband's wit, Miriam forged ahead in her work. When she had finally succeeded in restoring the alphabetical sequence, she revealed her plan: "I'm going to write a letter to every Adler in the book. One of them has got to be related to us, or at least sympathetic to a namesake. I'm sure someone will help."

"I've heard that assurance from you before," Moshe commented wryly, "and I caution you to reconsider. Strangers aren't going to respond to a Yiddish letter from someone they never met, even if they share our last name."

"Have you got a better idea?" she snapped back with a lump in her throat. "I know I shouldn't complain, but we've sold everything we own. I haven't made decent Shabbos in months, or eaten a square meal in weeks. What do you propose?!"

Before he knew it Moshe was also crying, and not long after that he was helping his wife hand-duplicate letters. For the next forty-eight hours, the Adlers did not see the light of day. As long as their eyelids could stay open and their fingers could move, they pressed on in their epistolary endeavor. On the morning of the third day, their job was finally complete and they commenced the laborious, tedious, and costly procedure of mailing the letters or dispatching them via whatever underground route was available. Many were sent with sailors who were bribed to mail them from distant countries.

IRONICALLY, when their mission had been accomplished they were curiously unrelieved. The project had managed to blissfully distract them from their bleak plight. In the last three days, it seemed that life had deteriorated significantly: food was scarcer than ever and it was rumored that even more restraints would soon be clamped upon the Jews. To appease the German government, Prime Minister Kallay had already instituted insufferable restrictions and forced-labor conscriptions. Still, the Nazis were implacable and demanded that all the Jews be "resettled" immediately in Poland.

Like their brethren in Vac and throughout Europe, the Adlers were desperate. The mail was their only hope of salvation, and it dominated their every prayer and thought. Eventually a few responses did start to trickle in — four, to be precise. Two of them were sympathy letters and two contained a grand total of seven dollars and best wishes. But that was it. Even Miriam Adler, the consummate optimist, despaired of deliverance arriving through the post.

I N FEBRUARY 1944, just four months before Auschwitz and Birkenau constructed additional railroad tracks and introduced extra shifts to "accommodate" Hungarian Jewry, a package arrived at the door of Moshe and Miriam Adler. Miriam's hopes soared. "Maybe Goldie sent us something we can sell!"

Moshe ripped open the package only to discover... a music box!

His disappointment and despair knew no bounds. "How in Heaven's name can this help us?" And without so much as a token moment of music appreciation, he hurled it against the wall with all the might remaining in his emaciated body.

The toy exploded into endless springs, dozens of gears, meters of wire, splinters of wood, chips of paint, and...

There was silence in the room, as both Moshe and his wife stared at the wreckage. There, underneath the rubble of wood and wire, were scraps of heavy paper and glinting coins.

Together, they lunged for the ruins. "Money!" Miriam cried.

"And certificates of passage for us and our

children!" Moshe's voice quavered with emotion.

"Look, there's a note."

Slowly, carefully, Miriam smoothed the crinkled piece of paper and read:

To Moshe and Miriam Adler:

I pray that you find the secret of this box before it is too late. I was told this was the safest route to take. Hopefully, I've enclosed everything you need to leave for New York. There, I will try to do for you all that you did for me.

Your friend and butcher,

Yitzchak Adler

THE ADLERS' sojourn in Hell ended on February 24, 1944. With the help of Yitzchak's papers and money, they were able to flee Vac and sail to New York. The quiet *seudas predah* they made for themselves was the last one Vac was to see before Germany invaded Hungary in March 1944.

From then till February 1945, more than 450,000 Jews living in and around Hungary were exterminated.

May the Lord avenge their blood.

Heard from: Mr. Joseph Weinstein

Glossary

The following glossary provides a partial explanation of some of the foreign words and phrases used in this book. The spelling, tense, and definitions reflect the way the word or phrase is used in *Pichifkes*. Often, there are alternate spellings and meanings for the words. Foreign words and phrases translated in the text are not included in this section.

AIBISHTER – (Yid.) God

AM HA'ARETZ – ignoramus

AMALEK – nation bent on the destruction of the Jewish people throughout history

BAALEI BATTIM – lay individuals

BAIS YOSEF – 1. Rabbi Yosef Karo; 2. his commentary on *Tur Shulchan Aruch*

BALABUSTA – homemaker

BAR MITZVA – 1. thirteen-year-old Jewish boy who assumes the religious responsibilities of an adult; 2. the ceremony confirming a bar mitzva

BARUCH HASHEM – lit. the Lord is blessed; thank God
B'CHVODO UV'ATSMO – "the one and only"
BENTCHING – reciting the grace after meals
BRIS – Jewish rite of circumcision
BROCH – (Yid.) blunder

CHALLAH – special loaves eaten on SHABBOS
CHANUKAH – the Festival of Lights
CHASSID(IM) – devout follower of a REBBE
CHAZZAN – cantor
CHEREM – excommunication
CHESSED – acts of lovingkindness
CHOLENT – stew traditionally eaten on SHABBOS
CHUPAH – 1. wedding canopy; 2. the wedding service
CHUSHEVEH – (Yid.) important

DAHEIR – (Yid.) comprehend
DAVEN – (Yid.) pray
DERASHAH – sermon

EIN YAAKOV – compendium of homiletical material
found in the Talmud
EMUNAH – faith
ERETZ YISRAEL – the land of Israel
EREV SHABBOS – Sabbath eve
GAON(IM) – lit. brilliant one; honorific for a
distinguished sage
GEDOLIM – outstanding Torah scholars
GEMARA – 1. commentary on the MISHNA (together
they constitute the Talmud); 2. a volume of the
Talmud
GESHMAK – (Yid.) sweet

HAKADOSH BARUCH HU – the Holy One, blessed be He

HAKAFOS – (pl.) circuits made with a Torah scroll on SIMCHAS TORAH

HAKKARAS HATOV – gratitude, appreciation

HALACHA – Jewish law

HAMENTASCHEN – triangular pastry traditionally eaten on PURIM

HASHEM – lit. the Name; respectful reference to God

HASHGACHA – Providence

HAVDALAH – lit. separation; prayer recited over wine at the conclusion of SHABBOS

HEILIGEH – (Yid.) holy

HEIMISH – (Yid.) homey

IBN EZRA – twelfth-century Biblical commentator

KAPOTA – traditional black frock worn by CHASSIDIM

KASHRUS – Jewish dietary laws

KEHILOS – communities

KIDDUSH – lit. sanctification; prayer recited over wine to usher in the Sabbath and festivals

KIPAH – skullcap

KISHKE – (Yid.) stuffing

KLAL YISRAEL – the community of Israel; all Jewry

KOLLEL – post-graduate yeshiva composed of young married students who receive stipends

KRECHTZ – (Yid.) mournful sigh

KUGEL – potato pudding

KVATER – (Yid.) person who brings the baby to his BRIS

KVETCH – (Yid.) complain

LAGERFUEHRER – camp commander

LAMDAN(IM) – scholar

LATKES – (Yid.) potato pancakes traditionally served on CHANUKAH

L'CHAIM – lit. to life; traditional toast

LEHAVDIL – to differentiate

MA NISHTANA HALAILA HAZEH MIKOL HALAILOS – lit. how is this night different from all other nights; question asked at the SEDER

MAHARSHA – Rabbi Shmuel Edels, sixteenth-century Talmudic commentator

MAIDELEH – (Yid.) girl

MAISSIM TOIVIM – good deeds

MASHGIACH(IM) – KASHRUS inspector

MASHGIACH TIMIDI – round-the-clock inspector

MAZEL – luck

MEIN – (Yid.) my

MELAMED – teacher

MENACHEM AV – eleventh month of the Hebrew calendar

MESHUGEH – crazy

MESIRUS NEFESH – dedication, devotion

MIKVA(OS) – ritual bath used for purification

MILAH – Jewish rite of circumcision

MINCHA – the afternoon prayer service

MINYAN – quorum of ten adult Jewish males; the basic unit of community for certain religious purposes, including prayer

MISHNA – the earliest codification of the Oral Law, by Rabbi Yehuda HaNasi

MISHNAYOS – sections of the MISHNA

MITZVA(OS) – commandment

MOHEL – one who performs the religious ceremony of circumcision

MORAI VE-RABBOSAI – my mentors and gentlemen

MUSSAR – admonishment

NEDER – vow, oath

NUDNICKS – (Yid.) pests

OY VEY – (Yid.) expression of woe

PARNASSA – livelihood

PASKEN – rule on halachic queries

PERUSH – commentary

PILPUL – Talmudic sophistry

POSEIK – halachic authority

PULKA – (Yid.) chicken leg

PURIM – joyous festival commemorating salvation from genocide

RACHMANA LITZLAN – (Aramaic) Heaven help us

RASHI – eleventh-century Biblical and Talmudic commentator

RAV – rabbi

REBBE(IM) – 1. rabbi; usually a Talmud teacher; 2. instructor; 3. chassidic leader

REBBETZIN – rabbi's wife

RECHOV – street

RIBBONO SHEL OLAM – Master of the universe

ROSH CHODESH – the new moon

SEDER – Passover ceremony commemorating the

Exodus from Egypt

SEFER (SEFARIM) – book of religious content

SEUDAH – festive meal

SHABBOS – the Sabbath

SHAILAH – halachic query

SHAIMOS – lit. names; repository for discarded written material containing God's name

SHALOM – peace

SHALOM ALEICHEM – lit. peace be unto you; traditional greeting

SHEITEL – wig worn by a married woman

SHEMA – lit. hear; prayer proclaiming the oneness of God and affirming faith in Him and His Torah

SHEMINI ATZERES – festival immediately following SUKKOS

SHIUR(IM) – Torah lecture

SHOCHET(IM) – ritual slaughterer

SHOMER SHABBOS – Sabbath-observant

SHTETL – (Yid.) village

SHTREIMEL – (Yid.) round, flat fur hat worn by CHASSIDIM

SHUCKLE – (Yid.) sway

SHUL – (Yid.) synagogue

SHULCHAN ARUCH – lit. set table; the Code of Jewish Law

SIDDUR(IM) – prayerbook

SIMCHA – lit. joy; celebration

SIMCHAS TORAH – festival concluding SUKKOS

SUKKOS – week-long autumn festival during which one dwells in a booth

TA'AM GAN EDEN – the taste of paradise

TACHLIS – (Yid.) "brass tacks"

TALLIS – four-cornered shawl with fringes at each corner, worn by men during morning prayers

TALMID – student

TALMUD TORAH D'RABBIM – public Torah study

TAMMUZ – tenth month of the Hebrew calendar

TEHILLIM – psalms; Book of Psalms

TESHUVA – repentance

TICHELACH – kerchiefs worn by married women

TISHREI – first month of the Hebrew calendar

TREIF – (Yid.) lit. torn; non-kosher; unacceptable

TZAAR BAALEI CHAIM – cruelty to animals

TZADDIK – righteous person

TZADDEKES – righteous woman

TZIMMES – glazed carrots

TZITZIS – fringes worn by males on a four-cornered garment

VAAD HAKASHRUS – KASHRUS council

VAAD HARABBANIM – rabbinical council

YEMACH SHEMAM VE-ZICHRAM – "may their name and memory be blotted out"

YID(IN) – (Yid.) Jew

YIDDISHEH NESHAMAH – (Yid.) Jewish soul

YIDDISHKEIT – (Yid.) Judaism

YINGEL – (Yid.) boy

YOM TOV – holiday

YUNGERMAN – (Yid.) young married man

ZECHUS – merit

Z"L – abbreviation for "of blessed memory"

Thousands of avid subscribers all over the world are raving about *StoryLines* — the new periodical for the entire family.

Here's Why:

Each inspiring tale in *StoryLines* is an original gem written by the king of storytellers, **Hanoch Teller**, whose stories have thrilled and uplifted Jewish audiences for over a decade.

Attractively designed and produced on high-quality paper, each issue contains a timely story about the holiday it heralds. Acclaimed by parents and educators alike, every issue of *StoryLines* includes: a feature length story annotated with a vocabulary-expanding glossary, a biography of a *tzaddik* or *tzaddekes* for teenagers, an easy-to-read tale for beginners, a cartoon episode of "Velvel the Wagon Driver," a parents' and teachers' guide for effective use of all the material, and much more.

StoryLines subscribers can take advantage of spectacular savings on books and cassettes not available elsewhere.*

Join the *StoryLines* sensation and receive a delightful "story-letter" three times a year: Rosh Hashana, Chanukah, and Purim. It's entertaining, intriguing, informative, and educational. You'll cherish every word. Subscribe today — don't be left out!

---

*Available only through subscription. Just $6.00 ($7.50 CAN/£ 3.50) for a one-year subscription.
37 West 37th St., 4th Fl., NY, NY 10018• 3 Prince Charles Dr. Toronto, Ont. M6A 2H1
127 Woodstock Ave. London NW11 9RL • Arzei Habira 46/7 Jerusalem 97 761